NOT ASHAMED

By the same Author:

NOT ASHAMED

Studies in Mission and Ministry

by

DOUGLAS WEBSTER

The Moorhouse Lectures
delivered in Melbourne 1969

HODDER AND STOUGHTON

COPYRIGHT © 1970 BY DOUGLAS WEBSTER

FIRST PRINTED 1970

ISBN 0 340 12814 3

Printed in Great Britain
for Hodder and Stoughton Limited,
St. Paul's House, Warwick Lane, London, E.C.4,
by Richard Clay (The Chaucer Press), Ltd.,
Bungay, Suffolk

To students and colleagues
at the Selly Oak Colleges
Birmingham, 1966–9
and especially
Norman Goodall
Paul Rowntree Clifford
Verleigh Cant

CONTENTS

PREFACE

It was a great privilege to be invited by the Archbishop of Melbourne and the Moorhouse trustees to deliver the Moorhouse Lectures in July 1969. To visit Australia at any time is a joyful experience. To be entertained and given hospitality by Archbishop Frank Woods and Dr. Robin Sharwood, Warden of Trinity College, Melbourne, where five of the lectures were delivered, was a sheer delight. To both of them and to the many clergy and students who gave me so much help, encouragement, and friendship, I must express deep gratitude.

The first six chapters of this book are the Moorhouse Lectures almost exactly as they were given. The seventh is the Bishop Jones Memorial lecture, which I had the honour to give at Carmarthen and Wrexham in February 1969 at the invitation of the Church Missionary Society. Although it is a singleton, I prepared it at the same time as I was working on the Moorhouse Lectures and it provides the conviction out of which they grew.

Most New Testament references are from the New English Bible and Old Testament references are from the Revised Standard Version.

The Moorhouse Lectures were given under the general title 'Interpreting the Lordship of Christ Today'. A book requires a shorter title. As the underlying theme throughout is the Gospel, how it is to be communicated and interpreted today, it seemed good to have a title which alludes to this. While I believe that there is much in the Church that needs changing and much of which we are deeply ashamed, like St. Paul I can still say of the Gospel—I am not ashamed.

I acknowledge with gratitude the permission of Mrs. Collins to quote from *Le Milieu Divin* by Teilhard de Chardin.

It may be of interest to remark that the opening paragraph of the introduction was written weeks before I had the least notion that the lecture itself would be delivered only eight hours after the American astronauts had walked on the moon. In Melbourne we watched this marvellous and breath-taking scene at 11 a.m. on Monday 21 July.

DOUGLAS WEBSTER

St. Paul's Cathedral
21 October 1969

INTRODUCTION

ON Christmas morning 1968 many of us woke up to hear the voice of an American from lunar orbit. He was reading from the first chapter of Genesis. On the same day we heard the Christmas Gospel: 'In the beginning was the Word, and the Word was with God, and the Word was God ... And the Word became flesh and dwelt among us.' On 6 January 1969 *The Times* published a magnificent colour picture of earth photographed from over the moon, quoting from Keats: 'Then felt I like some watcher of the skies when a new planet swims into his ken...' That same day, Christians celebrated the Feast of the Epiphany and remembered the story of star-led chieftains bringing their gifts to the infant Christ. This coincidence of supreme scientific achievement with the season when Christians rejoice in God's supreme gift to the human race confronts us with a double wonder: it also raises for many the ultimate questions about time and space, life and eternity, faith and meaning.

One of the earliest affirmations Christians made is expressed in three English words: 'Jesus is Lord!' (1 Cor. 12. 3). The Greek has two words only: Lord Jesus. From the first it was a confession of personal faith. St. Paul could speak of 'Christ Jesus my Lord' (Phil. 3. 8). But it was also a conviction of universal fact. Jesus was not merely Lord of the heart; he was Lord of the universe, Lord of all, sharing in the sovereignty of God. All things are to be subjected to him (1 Cor. 12. 27; Heb. 2. 8); all things are to be united and summed up in him (Eph. 1. 10); and every tongue is to confess that 'Jesus Christ is Lord' (Phil. 2. 11).

This belief is the bedrock of the Christian religion. On it Christianity stands or falls, the Church survives or disappears. But it is not sufficient to state or even to shout the Christian position to our world with its exploding population, its hungers, its tyrannies, wars, and revolutions. The declaration that Jesus is Lord has to be interpreted. What does this mean in the six continents, in the growing gap between rich and poor nations, in a pluralist society, both racially and religiously, in the artist's studio and the research laboratory, on the theatre stage, and the factory floor? How can we assert that Jesus is Lord today? This is the haunting question that prompts these lectures and suggests their theme and title. It would be absurd to pretend that the lectures will provide a set of answers. All that can be attempted is the exploration of some clues, the examination of some approaches, and the elimination of certain false assumptions.

Our main concern will be to consider what kind of responsibility belief in the Gospel and Lordship of Christ lays upon the Church at this time. We shall look at this in terms of two familiar, but often misunderstood, concepts: mission and ministry. The Gospel implies both, gives its own shape to both, and commits us to both. But today profound changes are affecting the forms of mission and the patterns of ministry which for so long have suffered from too narrow and professional an interpretation. For mission is infinitely more than the occupation of missionaries, and ministry is infinitely more than the occupation of clergy. To some extent they overlap, but each retains its own distinctive meaning. Both alike take their origin from Jesus Christ.

Before setting out on this line of study, there are certain hard facts to be noted. First, we are living at a time of Christian decline. This may be seen in numbers and in influence. At present some 30 per cent of the world's population is nominally Christian. By the end of this century it is expected that only 20 per cent will be Christian in a population which will have more than doubled.

Second, one of the features of today, more strongly marked than ever before and especially among the young, is a refusal to tolerate social injustice. The fact that 20 per cent of mankind enjoys 80 per cent of the world's wealth now disturbs the consciences of many people. It challenges the Churches for complacency and complicity in such a situation and while not changing the *esse* of the Christian mission it certainly sets it in a new and uncomfortable context. A further cause of Christian embarrassment is that most of the wealth is in the hands of white races, western nations, and peoples who largely profess to be the inheritors of Christian civilisation.

Third, until this century it was customary to think of the Christian frontier in geographical terms, and it was almost identical with the frontier between western civilisation and the rest of the world, most of which was under western imperial rule. Western dominance of this kind came to an end in Asia in 1947, in Africa in 1960. There are now strong Christian churches in places which were heathen a century ago, and heathendom is now in what once was Christendom.

Fourth, for a number of Christians, especially in North America, God is dead—that is, he has died as one with meaning for them and they can no longer use the word God. But for millions adhering to other faiths, Jews, Muslims, Hindus, God is convincingly alive. This led Kenneth Cragg to remark drily that 'the death of God is not to be unilaterally announced'. Thus, while there has been a steady retrenchment of Christian mission, there has been a remarkable advancement of other religious missions claiming the allegiance of men.

Fifth, many countries, once the sphere of dedicated missionary activity, have, over the last few years erected No Entry signs. This began with China in 1950. Sudan and Burma followed in 1965 and 1966. India, Malaysia, and Ceylon have not closed their doors but they have severely restricted the numbers of those they admit, and there are other countries following a similar policy. How does the Church discharge its mission without missionaries?

Sixth, there is in many circles a general malaise about any form of Christian mission in our day, and even among those deeply committed to it there are misgivings and doubts. These are voiced by a missionary leader: 'If you still believe in the worldwide relevance of Jesus Christ and are consequently making his message your business, you must expect to go on being confused, tempted to give up, and compelled to re-think for many years to come. And if you have not started to feel these misgivings and occasional losses of nerve about the missionary enterprise and your own part in it, then I can only infer that you have managed to get by without looking at the real world for a remarkably long time. The task which is laid upon us is the same as it has always been. But we are having to learn to see it in such utterly different perspective that the task itself sometimes seems to have changed' (John V. Taylor, *CMS News-Letter*, Nov. 1968).

With these hard facts and changed perspectives in mind we turn to the subject of our first lecture.

I. CONSIDER JESUS

WHEN questions about meaning are asked—and these are the most frequent questions today—it is usual to seek answers in the latest and most authoritative pronouncements. In religious and theological matters the obvious sources are reports from the World Council of Churches in Geneva or the documents of the Second Vatican Council in Rome. What is the most recent word on communicating the Gospel or re-modelling the missionary work of the Church? Where is wisdom to be found? While not casting doubt on the value of a good deal that emanates from these noble cities and the scholars whose writings influence their thought, I want to suggest another starting point. It is based on a telling phrase in the Epistle to the Hebrews: 'Consider Jesus, the apostle and high priest of our confession' (Heb. 3. 1 R.S.V.). The first part will be sufficient for our purposes: *Consider Jesus, the apostle.* It is surprising how little attention has been paid to this remarkable expression. Jesus the high priest is a familiar concept and the epistle to the Hebrews develops it, but only here in the whole of the New Testament is the title apostle given to Jesus. Jesus is *the* apostle *par excellence.* However vast the difference between the first and the twentieth century, all thinking about mission and ministry, as about Gospel, must begin with a consideration of Jesus. Apart from him there would be no Gospel, no mission, no ministry, and of course, no Church.

The main question which this lecture will try to examine is: What is mission? Immediately, as so often with the English language, we are up against the difficulty of vocabulary. No concordance or biblical word-book includes the words mission or missionary. They are not in the Bible. Their first appearance in English speech and writing was at the very end of the sixteenth century and they became more common in the seventeenth century. Nevertheless, both are derived from the Latin verb, to send. The Greek New Testament employs two verbs for send: *apostello* and *pempo*. They seem to be interchangeable, especially in the fourth Gospel, but the first of these has been transliterated in English to provide us with apostle, apostolate, apostleship. Unfortunately the noun form, *apostle*, has become almost a theological-technical term, largely confined to 'the Twelve' and a few others such as Paul and Barnabas, whereas originally it meant anyone sent with a message or dispatched on a mission. It is therefore in this family of words that we have to look for the meaning of mission, and we can welcome the increasing use of such phrases as 'lay apostolate' and 'apostolic Christians' in recent Roman Catholic writing. The Church is not apostolic because it is founded on the teachings of the twelve apostles. It is apostolic because—and in so far as—it shares in what Jesus embodied and the twelve continued, God's mission to mankind. The norm for understanding mission cannot in the last analysis be the findings of missionary councils or the achievements of missionaries. We see it as we consider Jesus, the apostle. In him God's mission to men is perfectly expressed and summed up. He is what God means by mission. He is its *esse*. All subsequent mission stems from him. In him the whole theology of mission is made explicit, as is its cost. He is *the* apostle, *the* missionary.

A word very closely related to mission is ministry. Although the meanings and derivations of these two words are quite distinct they can be used almost as equivalents in certain contexts. For example, the mission of Jesus and the ministry of Jesus mean much the same thing, and it would be hard to find any significant difference between the Church's mission to the world and the Church's ministry to the world. In these contexts both words are used functionally. But strictly speaking, ministry implies a certain status as well as function, the status of responsible servanthood. To this extent it qualifies the idea of mission; mission must take place in ministerial form. The person who is sent on a mission—and this applies as much in secular usage—is always the servant of the one who sends, whatever his importance and seniority in the community. The concept of ministry will occupy us in the next two lectures but we refer to it here because for Jesus mission and ministry are virtually synonymous and indistinguishable. Whereas today it is possible to have a sense of mission without ministry or to have a call to ministry without a sense of mission, this would have been unthinkable for Jesus and the early Church.

In the sermon in the synagogue at Nazareth, Jesus chose a passage which set out the programme of his ministry or, if you like, the content of his mission. Here was the manifesto of what he would seek to do and by implication the way he would seek to do it (Lk. 4. 18, 19). We shall look at it in more detail in the next lecture but now we may notice the strong sense of mission Jesus felt as he entered public life. He quotes the words: 'He has *sent* me.' Jesus is God's apostle. Later in this same chapter of Luke, when having been rejected at Nazareth he moved to Capernaum and found much more response, he said, 'I must give the good news of the kingdom of God to the other towns also, for this is what I was *sent* to do' (Lk. 4. 43). In the synoptic gospels there are only two other passages where Jesus speaks of being sent. There is the Lukan saying at the sending out of the seventy: 'Whoever listens to you listens to me; whoever rejects you rejects me. And whoever rejects me rejects the One who *sent* me' (Lk. 10. 16 with partial parallels at Mk. 9.37 and Mt. 10.40. T. W. Manson regards these three as all forms of one and the same original saying, see *The Sayings of Jesus* (London, 1949, p. 78). And there is the Matthaean logion: 'I was *sent* to the lost sheep of the house of Israel, and to them alone' (Mt. 15. 24). In all these verses the verb is *apostello*. There is also the parable of the wicked husbandmen in all the synoptists where the lord of the vineyard sends his beloved son (Mk. 12. 6; Mt. 21. 37; Lk. 20. 13. It is interesting to find that Luke here uses *pempo* while Matthew and Mark use *apostello*). This emphasis on God's sending of Jesus clearly goes back to his own teaching. Its theological developments which we find in Paul— 'God sent his own Son' (Gal. 4. 4)—and yet more in John— 'the Father sent the Son to be the saviour of the world' (1 Jn. 4. 14)—are entirely legitimate interpretations of the Lord's understanding of his mission. It is necessary to point this out because today there is a tendency to play down any

sense of divine mission Jesus may have had, and to regard
him as a religious pioneer who discovered what it meant to
co-operate with what God is doing in history. This has led
to popular reappraisals of contemporary Christian mission
primarily as recognition of God being at work in the movements of our time and seeing Christian apostleship as joining in. Jesus is more than this and so is his mission.

In an age when so many things, including mission, are
thought of globally and every enterprise is expected to have
a global strategy, it is a salutary corrective to realise how
local and limited the mission of Jesus was. In length it was
not more than three years and in area it was hardly one
hundred miles. Its scope was confined to the lost sheep of
the house of Israel and he studiously avoided involvement
in a mission to Gentiles. The time of the Gentiles could
only follow the Cross and the Resurrection (see J. Jeremias,
Jesus' Promise to the Nations, London, 1958, pp. 38, 72) for,
in the striking phrase of P. T. Forsyth, 'it was Christ's holy
death that catholicised his life' (P. T. Forsyth, *Missions in
State and Church*, London, 1908, p. 18). But the actual
mission of Jesus was profoundly limited and concentrated.
In a short period of time and a small area of space there
was united in one man a love for God and a love for the
world never known before. Out of this concentration came
the logic of his Cross and the universal range of his mission.
Do we not need to recover a sense of the local and the
limited before we think in terms of the global and the
strategic? Most of the things that come to be universal in
their effects begin at the local level in one place, whether
they be the discovery of penicillin, the writing of a pop
song, or an experiment in community. The local has to
impinge upon the universal before the universal can influence the local. Not until the congregation is structured
and trained for mission can a national Church be very
effective in mission. It is impossible fully to measure the
extent which some local imagination or initiative or obedience can reach. The Samaritans, the Bible Reading Fellowship, the Little Brothers of Jesus, the Parish Communion,
the East Harlem Protestant Parish, Alan Walker's Lifeline
in Sydney, Iona, Taizé, the Sheffield Industrial Mission, all
began on a small scale in one locality. But their effects have

spread far beyond the locality of origin. If John Wesley said 'the world is my parish', there is a sense in which we ought to be able to say 'the parish is my world'—not with the intention of being parochial or provincial, but with a glad and philosophical acceptance of limitation, remembering what can happen to a grain of mustard seed. The temptation today is to want everything organised, unified, and coordinated on a massive scale, and there are many who believe that the future of the Christian mission must yield to this. Grandiloquent titles like 'World Mission' are less than realistic and seriously misleading because they usually refer to organisation rather than achievement. All the evidence points in the opposite direction. Mission is intensely personal, being expressed in a web of human relationships and a host of tiny initiatives; it cannot be computerised like big business. Jesus is Lord, but the mission he undertook was on a very small scale and no-one called him Lord while he was engaged on it. Consider Jesus, the apostle.

In considering Jesus we must take into account the mode of mission which he exemplifies. There are six aspects which call for attention: these are presence, service, proclamation, training, healing, liberating. We will look at each in turn. First, mission presupposes presence. There can be no mission without presence because mission is personal and its agents are persons. In the history of Israel, when God wanted to make known his will in particular situations, he sent (or raised up) persons such as Moses and the prophets. When the fulness of time came he sent his Son. In the Christ-event a new stage was reached in the divine mission. Formerly the divine presence had been symbolised by the ark and confined to the Holy of Holies. Now the divine presence is made known in a man, for as St. Paul puts it, 'it is in Christ that the complete being of the Godhead dwells embodied' (Col. 2. 9). Formerly the divine Word had come through the prophets 'in fragmentary and varied fashion' (Heb. 1. 1), but now the Word has become flesh and dwelt among us (Jn. 1. 14). So God became incarnate in a particular human situation, circumscribed by time and space and knowledge, subject to severe human and physical limitations. Not until after his baptism in Jordan river did Jesus begin his mission, but orthodox Christianity does not teach that only then did he become divine. For some thirty years a God-filled man had been living in Nazareth but not engaging in any kind of public activity.

This suggests two things which bear on thinking about Christian presence as a mode of mission today. First, while all mission presupposes presence, presence does not necessarily presuppose mission. Second, mission is not something to be rushed into unprepared. By his presence in a situation for thirty years Jesus was preparing for a missionary venture which lasted only three. Presence is not in itself mission in the full sense of the word, which includes the conveyance of a message. But presence may well be a form of quiet witness and loving obedience in conditions which do not allow any kind of evangelism. Today there are many situations, especially in Marxist, Muslim, and Buddhist countries, where all that is possible is that groups of Christians should live and work and pray and help. At Nazareth, where Jesus was a working man, the divine presence was a reality but the divine mission was hidden. There cannot always be mission, but the Christ who promises to be in the midst of the two or three can always be present. Yet even where mission is permitted it is sometimes a dangerous and always a difficult undertaking and never more so than today. If the pattern of our Lord's life is in any way to be reflected in our modern methods it would seem to underline the strong need of preparation. To be present for a considerable time in missionary areas without engaging in mission may well be the only way to learn how to be effective and how to endure failure. Jesus knew both throughout. Despite this, there is always pressure to shorten and simplify the training both of ordained ministers and of missionaries, and there are some who would dispense with it altogether.

The second mode of mission in the ministry of Jesus was service. His life was lived for others. He gave himself. 'The Son of Man did not come to be served but to serve, and to surrender his life as a ransom for many' (Mk. 10. 45). 'If I, your Lord and Master, have washed your feet, you also ought to wash one another's feet' (John 13. 14). It is not enough to ritualise this in vestments whose symbolism is long forgotten or in ceremonies once a year on Maundy Thursday. We have to discover the modern equivalents of this ancient oriental gesture. They will vary from one place to another; what they will have in common is a willingness to do menial jobs and to get dirty. When Paul affirmed, 'We proclaim Christ Jesus as Lord, and ourselves as your servants, for Jesus' sake' (2 Cor. 4. 5), he showed his realisation that proclamation could never be divorced from service and that to announce the Lordship of Christ is to bind oneself to the service of all other men. Theoretically the Church recognises this but in practise it has often failed to hold the two together in its mission to the world, and large sectors of secular society have not yet seen enough Christian service to enable them to hear the Christian proclamation. With Jesus it was otherwise. For a time, at least, the common people heard him gladly because they felt he was the man for them and on their side. It was only when they discovered that his willingness to serve them did not mean subjecting himself to all their standards and desires that they joined in the rising opposition. Service is a way of loving one's neighbour, it is part of Christian behaviour, and it is one aspect of Christian mission. As an expression of love it is an end in itself, but it is not the only expression of love Christ had to offer and service alone did not convey all that he had to give.

This brings us to the third strand of Christ's mission, preaching. He had something to say. Mark's gospel (after a very brief introduction) puts this first: 'Jesus came into Galilee proclaiming the Gospel of God: "The time has come; the kingdom of God is upon you; repent, and believe the Gospel"' (Mk. 1. 14, 15). Undoubtedly this proclamation was at the heart of the mission of Jesus, even though there was more to his mission than this. We are entitled to use the attractive phrase popularised by John Robinson which speaks of Jesus as the Man for others, provided we are also prepared to regard him as the Man from God and the Man for God. We have already seen how conscious he was of being sent, not just of being called. He could speak authentically about God, telling men what he was like, what his purposes for them were, what he expected them to be and to do. He stressed the importance of decision, he appealed for commitment, he told of divine love and care, he promised deliverance or salvation, he implanted faith. Very

early on we read how 'the people were astounded at his
teaching, for, unlike the doctors of the law, he taught with
a note of authority' (Mk. 1. 22). John records a report of the
temple police to the chief priests and Pharisees: 'No man,'
they answered, 'ever spoke as this man speaks' (Jn. 7. 46).
Jesus spoke about God, and the good news he announced
was concerned with what God was like, what God was
doing.

In our generation we find it far from easy to speak about
God clearly and with conviction. David Edwards, criticising
certain theological statements made by Karl Barth, asks
pertinently: 'How dare he seem to be at home in the home
life of God?' (David L. Edwards, *Religion and Change*
(London, 1969), p. 353). This would probably be echoed by
many of us who lack the confidence of earlier generations
of preachers in being dogmatic about the eternal and tran-
scendent God. It is no bad thing that Christians should
admit that they cannot say everything that might be said
about God, or even that they cannot say anything like so
much as used to be said. But it would be a very bad thing
and a denial of the Gospel itself if Christians gave the
impression that they could no longer say anything at all
about God. Two of the theologians who have written most
helpfully on this subject are Ian Ramsey, Bishop of Durham, and David Jenkins. Jenkins writes: 'Jesus Christ is the
reality of man who confronts us with the reality of God.' It
is nothing like so difficult to speak about Jesus as it is to
speak about God. Jesus proclaimed the Gospel of God, but
the early Church proclaimed the Gospel of Christ. And this
was already implicit in what Jesus said about himself. Jesus
proclaimed himself, for he saw himself as embodying God's
Word and achieving his will. How else could he have issued
such invitations as 'Follow me ... Come to me ... Believe in
me'? If men are to believe in God they are most likely to
reach belief as he is presented to them in Jesus Christ.
Mission therefore cannot evade the proclamation of the
Gospel. How this can best be done raises many problems
some of which will occupy us later. At this point the concern is to notice the centrality of proclaiming the Gospel if
our mission is to be continuous with Christ's and to participate in God's.

Fourthly, Jesus engaged in training disciples. Training is perhaps a preferable word to teaching in this connexion. It included teaching but it led into group work, and the gospel narratives supply us with many a glimpse of the dynamics of the group. Again, unlike some teachers the approach of Jesus was not intellectual or cerebral. It was not programmed or systematic but spontaneous and arising out of real-life situations. Many an issue he never touched on. But he selected a band of men and allowed his own character and personality, his words and deeds, to make their impact on them and to refashion them. In his company they were to enter into a new life, to feel the powers of the Kingdom, to be born anew. They were to be changed so radically that one of them was promised a new name: 'You are Simon ... You shall be called Cephas' (Jn. 1. 42). He made enormous demands of them and yet he left them free. He called them initially to be with him, as in India the *guru* is surrounded by his pupils, but he also sent them out on their own, entrusting them with his message and his healing powers. Eventually he was to trust them with the future of his community, with its government and expansion. It is well known that the second part of Mark's gospel is almost entirely devoted to discipleship training, quite distinct from the earlier teaching of the crowd. (From Mk. 6. 30 and more particularly 8. 27 this becomes the predominant emphasis right through to the start of the passion.)

In this leadership training, as it would be called today, Jesus delegated authority and identified himself with the fortunes of the twelve: 'To receive you is to receive me' (Mt. 10. 40), 'whoever rejects you rejects the One who sent me' (Lk. 10. 16). One of the reasons why western missionaries have been under so much criticism in recent years, especially from the national leaders of their host churches, is that this pattern of training with its readiness to hand over power and authority and responsibility, has been followed too seldom and too late. As one who believes that there is still a place for the foreign missionary or fraternal worker in most churches, I believe also that many senior missionaries, however sincere and devoted, are obstructing the mission of the Church—not so much by refusing to train but by their unwillingness to trust those they have

trained. Jesus had no protective attitude to his trainees; he
let them make mistakes; he left them long before they fully
understood the. Gospel they were to proclaim; they were to
prove surprisingly obstinate and conservative in their relations with Gentiles and reluctant and slow to engage in a
Gentile mission, even after the Cornelius episode. In fact
the first leaders, the original twelve, seem never to have had
a missionary vision comparable to that which we find in
Paul and Barnabas and their friends. Nevertheless, Jesus
did not prolong his own period of teaching or show any
anxiety about the future of his little flock. Instead he
promised them the Holy Spirit who would teach them
everything and guide them into all the truth (Jn. 14. 23;
16. 13). Could one reason for the rapid growth of the Pentecostal Churches in Latin America be their reliance on the
Spirit rather than on a theological syllabus and academic
qualifications?

A fifth aspect of the mission of Jesus was his ministry of
healing. This was a pastoral ministry in the widest sense,
shown in a concern for healing at all levels. There are plenty
of instances of physical and mental healing. But Jesus
sought the healing of attitudes and of relationships. When
Zacchaeus resolved to make reparations for his financial
sharp practices Jesus said, 'Salvation has come to this house
today' (Lk. 19. 9). That was healing. 'If, when you are bringing your gift to the altar, you suddenly remember that your
brother has a grievance against you, leave your gift where it
is before the altar. First go and make your peace with your
brother' (Mt. 5. 23, 24). 'Love your enemies and pray for
your persecutors' (Mt. 5. 44). 'Always treat others as you
would like them to treat you' (Mt. 7. 12). These injunctions
are not just ethics. They are prescriptions for healing, they
are the mechanics of reconciliation. The Lord's teaching
about mutual forgiveness also comes into this category. 'If
(your brother) wrongs you seven times a day and comes
back to you seven times saying, "I am sorry", you are to
forgive him' (Lk. 17. 4). Likewise the experience of receiving
forgiveness and absolution is crucial to healing at any
depth, and it is significant that one version of the missionary command, in the setting of the first Easter, contains the
power to absolve or refuse absolution. 'If you forgive any

man's sins, they stand forgiven; if you pronounce them unforgiven, unforgiven they remain' (Jn. 20. 23). Being able to
express gratitude and say thank you is also therapeutic
according to Jesus; this was the significance of the tenth
leper (Lk. 17. 18, 19). In our day when courses are available
in clinical theology and counselling is often the modern
form of the confessional, we do well to remember that all
this is part of the ministry of healing and a vital mode of
mission.

A final aspect of mission as seen in Jesus we have called,
for want of a better word, liberating. Some modern writers
use stronger language, speaking of Jesus as the Outsider,
the Revolutionary, the Freedom Fighter (see Geoffrey
Ainger, *Jesus our Contemporary*, London, 1967, chapter 2).
I would not want to quarrel with these as useful images in
some contexts for communication purposes, but such titles
are so closely associated with anarchy and violence today
that it might be exaggerated as well as anachronistic to
apply them to Jesus. He did indeed say things which were
revolutionary. 'The Sabbath was made for the sake of man
and not man for the Sabbath' (Mk. 2. 27). Yet the revolutionary words of Jesus were not so much an abandonment
of earlier law as a much stricter interpretation of it. 'You
have heard that it was said to the men of old, "You shall
not kill; and whoever kills shall be liable to judgment". But
I say to you that everyone who is angry with his brother
shall be liable to judgment' (Mt. 5. 21, 22). He overturned
the money tables in the temple court and drove out the
merchants; he also called Herod Antipas 'that fox' (Lk.
13. 32). But he refused to start a rebel movement or to over-
throw the government in church or state, the one corrupt,
the other foreign and imperialist. He was however concerned with setting people free, giving them a chance to be
more human, resisting whatever made men less than men.
It was his teaching and ideas rather than his actions which
were revolutionary. Their time did not come for many a
century, but the things he said about man provided impetus
and energy for social revolutions of which we have only
seen the mere beginning. In the long run liberation from
various kinds of oppression was indeed to be a part of his
mission, and the Church, which in many countries occupies

so different a position from its founder, has opportunities to shape society and to alleviate the sufferings and privations of the masses which were never his but which are ours because of him. If the Church turns a blind eye to injustices around it, the world will turn a deaf ear to everything else the Church tries to say. Consider Jesus, the apostle.

Mission today should still have all these elements, whether it be the mission of the local congregation or the total witness of the Church in the life of the nation. Each unit of mission must constantly assess itself and its involvement with the secular world by weighing its concerns in these spheres. The only model for doing this is Jesus, the apostle.

II. MINISTRY IN THE NEW TESTAMENT

THE idea of priesthood is found in a number of religions in one form or other, but the idea of ministry is unique to Christianity. Other religions have some kind of professional class which acts in various ways between the deity and the people—there are the Brahmins of Hinduism, the mullahs or imams of Islam, the Buddhist monks, the priests and later the rabbis of Judaism. Their chief functions may include teaching the faithful, giving advice or judgment when required, and in some cases offering appropriate sacrifices. Their primary concern is not with any wider form of service. But the heart of the Christian Gospel is the concept of service or ministry. *Diakonia* can be translated by either word. 'The Son of Man did not come to be served but to serve' (Mk. 10. 45).

There are two sources of confusion which we must dispense with at once. First, the majority of discussions about ministry focus on the ordained ministry. This is not my intention here. So much has been written about 'the ministry', sometimes piously referred to as 'the sacred ministry', its origins, its forms, its emergence into episcopal and presbyteral, and the problems of church order in general, that it has been all too easy to forget the basic meaning and purpose of ministry and the sense in which this word was first understood by the early Christians. Failure in this respect has brought about some of the most perplexing problems facing the Church today. Just as in a certain type of 'catholic' theology in the past too great an emphasis on 'the faith', the content of what Christians believe, was at the expense of a sufficient stress on 'faith', *pistis*, the act of believing and of personal commitment to Christ, so too much concentration on 'the ministry', as an order within the Church, has led to a grave neglect of 'ministry', a function belonging to all Christian people. For in the New Testament ministry is an attitude long before it becomes an office. It was the

Christian way of looking at life and responding to the
world. It meant care as distinct from selfishness or indifference. It was based on the view that by acts of service
Christians could contribute to human progress, the coming
of God's kingdom and the doing of his will on earth as in
heaven, a view that was in marked contrast to the prevail-
ing determinism and submission to fate. Basically, ministry
is the Church turned outward to the world rather than its
internal organisation.

The other element of confusion arises from a natural
tendency to associate servanthood with social and class
structure. Normally a servant is regarded as an inferior, one
who has not made the grade and become his own boss. The
very phrase 'domestic service' conjures up a picture of
another world almost forgotten in the West and yet still
part of everyday life in Africa and Asia and even Eastern
Europe. (I could hardly conceal my surprise when on being
entertained to lunch by a German pastor in East Berlin we
were waited on at table by two maids.) But there is nothing
particularly degrading or derogatory in the servant concept
as we find it in the Bible. Even where the servant was a
slave in status he could hold high office, as the story of
Joseph in Egypt shows. The main features of servanthood
in the Old Testament, where the Hebrew word occurs some
800 times, are work, obligation, and obedience. Servanthood
signifies a relationship of responsibility. While much service
is menial this is not true of all forms of service. In our own
English language the word minister is not confined to
clergy; there are ministers of state, holding high office,
whose function is the service of the sovereign and of the
people. If therefore we choose to speak of a servant church
or a serving community we are not implying servility nor a
body of subservient, unprotesting people who do what they
are told. The Lord who took upon himself the form of a
servant never became servile and his humility had none of
the characteristics of Uriah Heep.

The phrase 'servant church', which we have just used, is
highly fashionable today. It is important to ask, Whose servant? The assumption is generally made that the Church is
called to serve the world, for does not the world write the
agenda, and is not the Church's task set by this agenda? So

runs a good deal of popular ecumenical thought. There is a lot of truth in this line of argument provided it is not over-stated, but we are in danger today of getting it out of pro-portion. For a corrective we need to turn to the New Testament. A number of Greek words are translated servant but for our consideration the two most important are *diakonos* and *doulos*. Of these *doulos* is far the more frequent. With *diakonos* the reference is primarily to function, that of waiting, attending, ministering, executing the command of another; but with *doulos* the reference is mainly to relationship, that of bondsman or slave, one who is altogether owned by someone else and who gives himself completely to the will of another. Obviously the Church is not related to the world in this way. St. Paul writes of being the *doulos* of sin (Rom. 6. 16 ff.) and the *doulos* of Jesus Christ (Rom. 1. 1; Gal. 1. 10). *Diakonos* can be used for the latter (Col. 1. 7) but not for the former. Jesus never used the noun *diakonos* or *doulos* of himself but each word is used once to describe him by Paul, who said that Christ became a *diakonos* to the circumcised (Rom. 15. 8) and took the form of a *doulos* (Phil. 2. 7). More commonly these words are used of Christians but generally in their relation to God or Christ or the Gospel. In Paul we find 'diakonoi of a new covenant' (2 Cor. 3. 6), 'diakonoi of God' (2 Cor. 6. 4), 'diakonoi of Christ' (2 Cor. 11. 23), 'diakonos of the Gospel' (Eph. 3, 7; Col. 1. 23) 'diakonos of the Church' (Col. 1. 25). A similar emphasis is given to *diakonia*, translated ministry or service. There is 'the ministry of the Spirit' (2 Cor. 3. 8), 'the ministry of righteousness' (2 Cor. 3.9), 'the ministry of reconciliation' (2 Cor. 5. 18), 'the ministry of the word' (Acts 6. 4).

My purpose in quoting these references is to indicate that in the New Testament period the notion of ministry was very firmly related to certain specific spheres of thought and had not come to be used, as it often appears to be today, to suggest a multi-service agency, responding to every request, rather like a continuing bob-a-job week but, of course, without the bob. We have already observed that not everything is mission; we must also urge that not everything is ministry. Too general and slipshod a use of *diakonia*, which is the present tendency, should be resisted. There is indeed a ministry to the world, a ministry of Christian people to all

people, which includes feeding the hungry, clothing the
naked, healing the sick, and other forms of social service.
All this is *diakonia* and it is grounded in the Gospel and in
the example of Jesus. But current use of *diakonia* too often
concentrates *exclusively* on its manward and social aspects,
forgetting that fundamentally this calling is to be servants
of God, of Christ, of the Gospel, and that one very important consequence of such ministry is the service of mankind. Putting this another way we might say that in the
New Testament *diakonia* is God-orientated before it is
directed towards men.

Nevertheless, just as love in its Christian sense must
always be to God and to neighbour, so also must ministry.
St. John asks: 'if any one has the world's goods and sees his
brother in need, yet closes his heart against him, how does
God's love abide in him?' And he goes on to assert that 'he
who does not love his brother whom he has seen, cannot
love God whom he has not seen' (1 Jn. 3. 17; 4. 20). A similar
duality exists in the case of ministry or service. In so far as
it is offered to God it must reach out to men and be concerned with all human need. In the Old Testament Moses is
portrayed as God's servant in a special sense, 'Moses, my
servant' (Nu. 12. 7; Josh. 1. 2). But this servanthood is expressed in the service of God's people. He leads them out of
slavery and brutal conditions into liberty and independence. The Bible sees no incompatibility between being a
leader and being a servant, for the ideal of leadership it
presents is always in servant terms. The Old Testament pre-
pares the way for the combination of Servant-Lord in the
Christ-figure of the New. This is vividly brought home
when Jesus girds himself with a towel and at the end of his
symbolic gesture says: 'Do you understand what I have
done for you? You call me "Master" and "Lord", and
rightly so, for that is what I am. Then if I, your Lord and
Master, have washed your feet, you also ought to wash one
another's feet' (Jn. 13. 12, 14). If we are right in seeing the
feet-washing episode as an acted parable of the Cross, interpreted as Christ's great cleansing action made available for
all humanity, we must assume that the washing of 'one
another's feet' is not something limited to the in-group of
Christians but is the way the followers of Jesus are intended

to behave towards humanity as a whole. This way of qualifying for leadership is recommended in another saying of
Jesus to the disciples. 'You know that in the world, rulers
lord it over their subjects, and their great men make them
feel the weight of their authority; but it shall not be so with
you. Among you, whoever wants to be greater must be your
servant (*diakonos*), and whoever would be first must be the
willing slave (*doulos*) of all—like the Son of Man; he did
not come to be served, but to serve, and to surrender his life
as a ransom for many' (Mt. 20. 25–8). Here, a sharp contrast
is drawn between worldly or secular forms of leadership and
the Christian way of using power over others. In the fine
words of T. W. Manson, 'In the Kingdom of God service is
not a stepping-stone to nobility: it *is* nobility, the only kind
of nobility that is recognised' (T. W. Manson, *The Church's
Ministry*, London, 1948, p.27). So ministry is defined as
being 'the willing slave of all' and this provides a key for
understanding the Church's relation to the world. The
apostle Paul makes use of the same paradox. He had many
of the leadership qualities and problems of Moses. In his
Corinthian correspondence we find him exercising authority in an uncompromising manner, refusing to be a tool or a
yes-man. Yet, in addition to calling himself the bond-ser-
vant of Jesus Christ (Rom. 11. 1), he goes so far as to refer to
all who hold the apostolic commission as 'ourselves your
servants (*doulous*) for Jesus' sake' (2 Cor. 4. 5). What does the
kind of ministry or service mean in practical terms? To
answer this we must return to the Lukan passage where
Jesus issued his manifesto of ministry in the synagogue at
Nazareth.

The words quoted from Isaiah may be analysed into five
strands which run through the whole of the New Testament and their context provides a sixth. They provide us
with the seminal ideas of all that ministry should mean.
There are occasional overlaps with what has already been
said about the Lord's mode of mission but we are looking at
it from another angle.

'The spirit of the Lord is upon me because he has anointed
   me;
He has sent me to announce good news to the poor,

To proclaim release for prisoners and recovery of sight for
    the blind;
To let the broken victims go free,
To proclaim the year of the Lord's favour' (Lk. 4. 18, 19).

The first strand is—in the full theological sense—Pentecostal. It is notable that in Luke's Gospel the first word that
Jesus utters in public is about the Spirit of the Lord (R.V.,
R.S.V., Moffatt and Phillips give a capital S against N.E.B.
and Jerusalem Bible where it is in lower case). St. Luke in
his capacity as a theologian, which modern scholarship increasingly recognises, is at pains to insist that all ministry is
a gift of the Spirit. Without the anointing of the Spirit
there can be no Christian ministry. Jesus did not and could
not begin his own ministry until after his baptism with the
Spirit. For him baptism was ordination, designation, commissioning, a setting free for ministry. Attention has often
been drawn to the significance of the words spoken by the
voice from heaven at the baptism. The first phrase 'thou art
my beloved Son' has a Messianic reference (Ps. 2. 7), and the
second phrase 'with thee I am well pleased' comes from the
first of the Servant Songs (Isa. 42. 1). Taken together they
presented Jesus with the polarity of his vocation and ministry, and in the Temptation narrative which immediately
follows he is seen to be working out how to interpret his
Messiahship in a way consistent with servanthood. But
Luke sets all this in a strongly Pentecostal framework.
At the baptism the Spirit descends on Jesus (3. 22); he
returned from the Jordan 'full of the Holy Spirit' and was
'led by the Spirit up and down the wilderness and tempted
by the devil' (4. 1). It is worth noting that being inspired
and being tempted can be simultaneous experiences. After
the temptation 'Jesus, armed with the power of the Spirit,
returned to Galilee' (4. 14), eventually going up to Nazareth
where he pronounced the words 'The spirit of the Lord is
upon me'. This is the context in which his ministry began
and evidently Luke expected all ministry to be initiated by
the gift and prompting of the Spirit. It is interesting to
notice that in the Moses saga, ministry is also associated
with the Spirit. When Moses found the leadership and
administration of the people too big a job to be carried

alone, the Lord said: 'Gather for me seventy men of the elders of Israel ... and I will take some of the spirit which is upon you and put it upon them; and they shall bear the burden of the people with you' (Nu. 11. 16 f.). These elders were not given a share in the work of Moses without a participation in the Spirit with which he was endowed. Ministry, as the Bible conceives it, is not something anyone can undertake at will.

In Luke's second volume, the Acts of the Apostles, his theme is the continuance of the ministry of Jesus through his Church. The disciples had been promised the Spirit and told to stay in Jerusalem until they were 'armed with the power from above' (Acts. 1. 8; Lk. 24. 49). They made no attempt to minister or even to speak in public until after the day of Pentecost when 'they were all filled with the Spirit ... and the Spirit gave them power of utterance' (Acts 2. 4). After that they could not help speaking (Acts 4. 20), and the immediate result of Pentecost was the proclamation of the deeds of God by the apostle Peter, the first recitation of the *kerygma*. At a later stage the inauguration of an entirely new missionary venture by the Church at Antioch was a direct response to the prompting and commissioning of the Spirit (Acts 13. 3, 4). There is not time to trace this Pentecostal strand through the letters of Paul but we may notice its prominence in 1 and 2 Corinthians, where in the first part of each letter he is particularly concerned with ministry. He claimed that although feeling frightened and inadequate when he came to Corinth his message had been 'in demonstration of the Spirit and power (1 Cor. 2. 4 R.S.V.). The impression conveyed is that by nature Paul was a reluctant preacher but that he was compelled to preach by the insistent Spirit. In the first five chapters of 2 Corinthians, for which the New English Bible's heading is 'Personal Religion and Ministry', there is a closely argued discussion about the place of the Spirit in the new covenant of which Paul is a minister (2 Cor. 3).

In the light of this intimate link between the Spirit and the ministry in the New Testament, we may feel it right to ask whether sufficient weight has been given to it in current discussions about ministry. One does not have to be a Pentecostalist to believe in Pentecost, but it is possible that many of the Churches will need to learn from the Pentecostalists before they recover a full doctrine of ministry. In the Ordinal the gift of the Spirit is deemed essential before the authorisation of men for certain ministries in the Church, and there is an increasing trend towards interpreting the rite of Confirmation as the ordination of the laity for their various ministries. But if in Anglican thinking the Spirit is largely confined to such services and to the laying on of hands, we are not likely to recover any of the excitement and wonder which the early Christians had—and which Pentecostalists still have—of that joint participation in the Spirit called *koinonia* in the New Testament, and creating the fellowship. Confirmation and ordination are formal occasions and happen only once. Fellowship is meant to be a continuous pattern of life. It is within the fellowship that the gift of the Spirit can be stirred into flame (2 Tim. 1.6) and true *diakonia* can be born only there.

The second strand in the Nazareth definition is the evangelistic. 'He has sent me to announce good news to the poor'. In answer to the enquiry by John the Baptist, 'Are you the one who is to come, or are we to expect some other?' (Mk. 11.3), Jesus sent the delegation to report on what they saw and heard, the final item of which was that 'the poor are hearing the good news'. Apparently Jesus felt a compulsion to preach the Gospel. 'I *must* give the good news of the kingdom of God to the other towns also' (Lk. 4.43). Luke uses the same Greek word, *dei*, for the passion predictions, 'the Son of man must suffer many things' (Lk. 9.22; 13.33), denoting logical necessity as distinct from moral obligation. So the preaching of the Gospel is seen as part of the logic of the Spirit. But before we follow this strand through it is worth asking what is meant by 'the poor'. Is not the Gospel for all men, including the rich? We cannot evade the difficulty by urging that this does not refer to material poverty, the economic poor, for the Lord showed special concern for them. Nevertheless, while in Luke's version of the beatitudes Jesus says 'Blessed are you poor', Matthew interprets this as 'Blessed are the poor in spirit' (Lk. 6.20; Mt. 5.3). Poverty in spirit suggests an openness, a sense of need and dependence, a willingness to receive and to have things done for one. In this sense there is a parallel between the poor and the children, to both of whom Jesus ascribes the Kingdom of God. In the Bible there is a poverty which cannot be measured in economic terms. 'You say, "How rich I am! And how well I have done! I have everything I want in the world." In fact, though you do not know it, you are the most pitiful wretch, poor, blind, and naked' (Rev. 3. 17). The Gospel therefore makes sense to those aware of what they lack. To all others it is either an insult or an irrelevance. Is not this the significance of the poor and the reason for the glorification of poverty understood as a disposition to receive?

In the apostolic Church, as we have seen, the preaching of the Gospel is the immediate consequence of Pentecost. There was the same sense of compulsion; the apostles were irrepressible. 'The lion has roared, who will not fear? The Lord has spoken, who can but prophesy?' (Amos 3. 8). 'We cannot possibly give up speaking of things we have seen and heard,' said Peter and John in the Jewish court (Acts 4. 20). They had to bear witness and this was evangelism. The same compulsion is seen in St. Paul, not only in his relentless preaching of the Gospel in Acts but in his own acknowledgment of this urge. 'Even if I preach the Gospel, I can claim no credit for it; I cannot help myself; it would be misery to me not to preach' (1 Cor. 9. 16). This sentiment is not always echoed today, when more often the misery is in having to preach! But we need not labour the point; we all admit its validity even if we shun the consequences. Unfortunately the concept of evangelism has acquired many overtones; it is associated with high pressure methods, with arrogance, aggressiveness, and a proselytising attitude. In many situations the news is no longer new, the story is indeed old and has died in the telling and re-telling. Evangelism has become the hardest and heaviest part of the Christian ministry. And yet, when we have allowed for all this, the fact remains that the Church's primary task is to proclaim the Gospel in each new generation and in every society. The Gospel is more than a cultural inheritance. It is an existential announcement about God to be addressed to all men everywhere. We must certainly find new ways of presenting it, avoiding the charge of being six foot above contradiction, accepting the challenge of dialogue, finding secular platforms and pulpits, translating it into contemporary images and idiom; but evangelise we must. It is every man's birthright to hear this good news about the God who made him and loves him and the destiny for which he was created. As Bishop Stephen Neill has reminded us: 'If no Christian goes to Japan, the Gospel will not be preached to the Japanese, and no Japanese will become a Christian. Whatever part the great Japanese civilisation is called to play in the purpose of God, it will not be a Christian part, unless very human Christians bestir themselves to make very human efforts, and pass on to others the good word that they themselves have received' (S. C. Neill, *The Church and Christian Union*, London, 1968, p. 101). It is as simple and as hard as that.

The third strand in Jesus' outline of ministry is social action. This relates to what was said in the first lecture about the liberating aspect of his mission. It is 'to proclaim release for prisoners ... to let the broken victims go free'. A generation ago people sometimes spoke of 'the social Gospel'. This is an unfortunate and misleading phrase. There is only one Gospel and it needs no adjectives. But just as it raises personal issues and requires personal response, so it raises social issues which demand social change. Although the immediate impact of Jesus was on individuals, in the long term he was to affect society enormously. One dramatic effect of the Gospel is illustrated in Paul's letter to Philemon where we see it radically altering the mutual relations between a master and a slave. The status of women and the sanctity of marriage, family, and home were influenced by it in the first decades and constantly since. An element of compassion was introduced towards all who were subject to any kind of oppression, misfortune, or victimisation. From a purely secular viewpoint how much poorer and crueller the world would have been but for Jesus! During his ministry in a land under foreign rule he was in no position to bring about reforms or to introduce enlightened and humane legislation, nor was the Church for a long time. But we see the rapid social consequences of the Gospel in action for the benefit of widows and orphans (Jas. 1. 27; Acts 6. 1; 1 Tim. 5. 3 ff.) and in Paul's concern for the Jerusalem poor (Rom. 15. 26). In our own day it is possible to trace a direct connexion between the rise of nationalism, especially in Africa, and the preaching of the Gospel a few generations previously, implying, as it did, a Christian view of man, of freedom, and of responsibility. In this respect missions can be proud at being charged with 'interfering in the secular' (see Norman Goodall, *Christian Missions and Social Ferment*, London, 1964, chapter 1). In the protestant parish of East Harlem this kind of social witness proved inescapable. 'There were those who held that all this involvement in problems of garbage, housing, police, and poverty was consuming time which would have been better spent in preaching the Gospel. The Group believed that this *was* preaching the Gospel ... They dare not spiritualise Christ's Gospel' (Bruce Kenrick, *Come Out of the Wilderness*, London, 1963, pp. 61, 52). This may seem a far cry from the much more limited social action in the early Church, but in a very different world it is a logical development of one conviction from the apostolic age, that religion means visiting the orphans and widows (Jas. 1. 27).

The fourth strand of ministry as Jesus envisaged it is healing—'recovery of sight for the blind'. We have already noted the place of healing in his own mission. This was to continue in the ministry of his followers. When the twelve were first sent out, in addition to proclaiming the message, he commanded them to 'heal the sick, raise the dead, cleanse lepers, cast out devils' (Mt. 10. 8). This is apostolic ministry, a programme which is an authentic ministry in itself. Healing in all its ranges can never be separated from the Gospel. In Acts we find the apostles engaged in healing and St. Paul speaks of 'the signs of a true apostle' which included wonders and mighty works (2 Cor. 12. 12; Rom. 15. 19; cf. Acts 5. 12; 19. 11 f.). The Church in our day sorely needs to recapture this form of ministry and once again to become a healing community

The fifth and final strand in the Nazareth manifesto is 'to proclaim the year of the Lord's favour'. The most surprising thing about this is that Jesus does not complete the quotation from Isaiah where the next item to be proclaimed is 'the day of vengeance of our God'. The Isaiah passage was understood as implying God's favour to Israel and his vengeance on those regarded as Israel's enemies.

But in the sermon which follows Jesus shows that God's favour also reached those who were outside Israel, Naaman the Syrian and the widow of Sarepta in Sidon. Thus Jesus expanded and revolutionised the whole concept of salvation. In effect he was denouncing racialism, tribalism, every kind of separateness; his sermon had a tremendous missionary thrust and for that reason, as not infrequently since, it infuriated the congregation. But his main point is that 'today in your very hearing this text has come true'. The year of the Lord's favour had arrived, and Jesus was to concentrate on grace, not vengeance. This was the here-and-now of salvation. Jesus spoke about the New and the Now, and it was this sense of immediacy which inspired and excited all his ministry.

In Acts the apostles proclaimed the new age, but they were slow in realising its full meaning, even after the Cornelius episode, the equivalent for them of Naaman the Syrian, but the full extent of God's favour came home to them when they had to confess: 'this means that God has granted life-giving repentance to the Gentiles also' (Acts 11. 18). They were startled by the novelty and immediacy of grace: it was new and it was happening now.

For St. Paul this concept is at the heart of his Gospel. 'When anyone is united to Christ, there is a new world; the old order has gone, and a new order has already begun' (2 Cor. 5. 17). He wrote these words out of a missionary experience which had seen people pass from the old to the new. And a little later in the same passage he quotes another verse from Isaiah: ' "In the hour of my favour I gave heed to you; on the day of deliverance I came to your aid". The hour of favour has now come; now, I say, has the day of deliverance dawned' (2 Cor. 6. 2). Once more we meet the New in the Now. This was the reality which made ministry possible, which provided its impetus. In the New Testament all ministry is energised by this sense of God's today, of being witnesses to the grace of God at work now. The letter to the Hebrews has a long exposition of the meaning of 'Today' in Psalm 95: 'Today if you hear his voice, do not grow stubborn.' The writer says, 'Day by day, while that word "Today" still sounds in your ears, encourage one another' (Heb. 3. 13). Christians engaged in ministry can always be expectant because they are living in God's 'Today', and there is no knowing what may happen and there are no limits to his grace.

The background to the Isaiah passage provides what we may take as the sixth, if basic, strand to ministry—the fact of servanthood, the status to be embraced if the functions are to be fulfilled. The word servant does not occur in the text and the text does not come from a servant passage. Nevertheless, its opening words are strongly reminiscent of two earlier affirmations in the book of Isaiah. The first is messianic: 'There shall come forth a shoot from the stump of Jesse ... and the Spirit of the Lord shall rest upon him' (Isa. 11. 1, 2). The second is from the first servant song: 'Behold my servant, whom I uphold ... I have put my Spirit upon him' (Isa. 42. 1). Before preaching at Nazareth, Jesus had been through the experiences of baptism and temptation in both of which, as we have seen, the messianic and servant ideas were prominent and partially in conflict. Jesus does not refuse Messiahship, but he does refuse to advertise it and he interprets it in suffering servant terms. For him ministry could never be mere servanthood; he saw that its final effectiveness would depend on suffering and sacrifice. His mission must lead into his Passion (Mk. 10. 45). Such was to be the pattern of ministry, the calling of the servant of God in the world of God in all ages. The point we must particularly notice is that those who want to do the work of God in this world cannot hope to get very far in sharing his mission unless they are content to share also in Christ's willingly accepted servant status. This is the condition for mission. Jesus took upon himself 'the form of a servant' (Phil. 2. 7), and this is the form Paul also took (1 Cor. 9. 19; 2 Cor. 4. 5; cf. Acts 26. 16). It is not inconsistent with the exercise of authority but it is always a derived authority, delegated by Christ, and therefore far more effective and powerful than any personal authority could be. We may recall the centurion's remark to Jesus, 'I am myself under orders with soldiers under me', implying that the validity of authority depends on its source. For the centurion the source was the emperor, and he assumed that likewise Jesus could act authoritatively because he was the servant of God (Mt. 8. 9).

Finally we must look at certain patterns, types, and varieties of ministry discernible in the New Testament. These will provide us with standards and principles by which we can attempt in the next lecture to assess ministry as we know it today. I would invite your attention to five points.

First, there was that great moment quite early on in the life of the apostolic community, when a crucial decision was made which led to a bifurcation in their interpretation of ministry. We refer of course to the crisis in Acts 6 over the Hellenist widows. This occurred during a period of rapid growth. When the complaint arose that this particular group was being neglected, the apostles were quick to recognise two things. On the one hand the Church could not divest itself of responsibility for the need of these people. On the other hand they, the twelve, could not personally undertake it. They found themselves forced to accept the principle of delegation, of a shared ministry, of a differentiation of function. The result was the appointment of the seven to look after these affairs while the apostles saw clearly that they must devote themselves to prayer and the ministry of the Word. This was not to imply that the seven were exempt from these activities for they engaged in both, two of them becoming very effective preachers, so there was no question of a superior and inferior ministry, one being more or less spiritual than the other. The qualifications for the seven were that they should be 'men full of the Holy Spirit and of wisdom'. The Spirit is required for every form of ministry in the New Testament. The real significance of this decision is that the apostles refused to become multi-functional. Christians in the New Testament period were not expected to offer every kind of service or to be the equivalents of general practitioners in the medical profession of recent times. The apostles distinguished between being ministers and administrators—a distinction too often forgotten by churches and clergy today—and they definitely opted for the former.

Second, an extension of this original diversity of function is worked out in the teaching and practice of St. Paul. He sees a great assortment of ministries related to the great assortment of spiritual gifts, *charismata*. 'There are varieties of gifts, but the same Spirit. There are varieties of service, but the same Lord' (1 Cor. 12. 4, 5). It is interesting to notice that gifts are associated with the Spirit and ministries with the Lord, that is Jesus. Paul lists the various ministries in two important passages (1 Cor. 12. 28–30; Eph. 4. 11. For this purpose I am not concerned with the authorship of Ephesians). In the one list they are those whom God has appointed in the Christian community; in the other they are the gifts of the ascended Christ to his Church. Paul sets out the *charismata* in two other passages (Rom. 12. 6–8; 1 Cor. 12. 7), insisting that 'in each of us the Spirit is manifested in one particular way, for some useful purpose', namely some desired ministry (1 Cor. 12. 7). No-one has all the gifts; no-one can fulfil all the functions of ministry. But both alike have been given 'to equip God's people for work in his service (*diakonia*) to the building up of the Body of Christ' (Eph. 4. 12). Here is a statement of the comprehensiveness and inclusiveness of the ministry of the people of God—and its ultimate aim. It is a gift within the Church to enable Christians to witness and work outside the Church, the goal being the completion of the Body of Christ. There is no contrast as yet between minister and people, *diakonos* and *laos*. All are God's people serving in God's world.

Third, in addition to differences of function the New Testament also recognises differences of spheres in ministry. This is evident from two other sets of distinctions. There is a distinction between itinerant ministries and local ministries. Apostles, prophets, evangelists, are certainly itinerant in the main. Pastors on the other hand are essentially local. Teachers might have been either but are more probably associated with a local congregation. The second distinction is between ministries done on behalf of the whole Church and therefore requiring official authorisation (ordination) and ministries which anyone could exercise voluntarily and spontaneously within a particular congregation or locality. Ministries of healing and counselling and general offers of help would fall into the latter category, while oversight of a congregation obviously came into the former and St. Paul *appointed* elders charged with this responsibility (Acts 14. 23; cf. Tit. 1. 5; 2 Tim. 2. 2). Here we may find the beginning of that division, which in history has become so exaggerated, between lay and ordained ministries in the Church, the ordained gradually acquiring a totality of active ministry and the lay for the most part being left as mere passive recipients.

Fourth, it is well known that in the early Church and for some centuries there was no extensive paid, full-time, professional ministry. The apostles were doubtless full-time and like the later bishops were supported by the offerings of the faithful, and deacons, who were part of the bishop's household, would normally be provided for by him. The early church devised special regulations for meeting the expenses of itinerants (see *The Didache*, xi–xiii), but presbyters earned their own living and gave their services voluntarily. It is possible that they were entitled to expenses or an honorarium (1 Tim. 5. 17). If this pattern had been followed in the churches resulting from the missionary movement of the nineteenth century we should have a different and more healthy situation today, as we shall seek to show. The main point to notice here is that in the New Testament ministry is basically voluntary; it is by no means confined to the very few full-time paid officials.

Finally, in the apostolic Church ministry is essentially a group activity. It is never seen as a solitary job and there is nothing monarchical about it. The apostles in Acts seem to have acted corporately as a college or council. In his relations with the Corinthian church Paul certainly used his apostolic authority, but he was writing to first generation Christians whose faith was the outcome of his own ministry among them (1 Cor. 3. 1–3, 10; 2 Cor. 11. 2). In modern times some pioneer missionaries have been in a position to use this kind of authority; but never their successors. In the second century there emerged the monarchical episcopate. Recently the Roman Catholic Church has moved away from this concept and made attempts to recover the idea of a *collegium*. Be that as it may, a far greater departure from the New Testament is the monarchical presbyterate which in one form or another in nearly every church and denomination has become the pattern and continued for centuries. Pastors have too often been domineering figures, despite explicit warnings about this by St. Peter (1 Pet. 5. 3).

Churches have been clericalist. There has also been a

long period of monarchical missionaries, though happily this has mostly passed. In the New Testament, however, we see St. Paul surrounded by a group of friends of both sexes, all engaging in ministry as a team effort.

We have selected these five items because later history has largely left them behind. Some would claim that the changes were legitimate developments; others would say that they were disastrous distortions. In the crisis of today we have to decide where the truth lies. That is our task in the next lecture.

III. MINISTRY TODAY

ONE of the recurrent images in the Bible is that of the shepherd. In the Old Testament the Israelites knew God as their shepherd long before they knew him as their Father. 'The Lord is my shepherd' was creed as well as song (Ps. 23. 1. cf. Ps. 80. 1; Isa. 40. 11; Jer. 31. 10). But kings and priests and prophets, the leaders of the people, were also shepherd figures Jeremiah and Ezekiel prophesy against 'the shepherds of Israel' (Jer. 23. 1; Ezk. 34. 2). The pastoral concept was not wholly religious, though it is certainly religious in origin. In the gospels Jesus is a shepherd figure. There are the sayings about lost sheep and sheep without a shepherd, and in the fourth gospel Jesus is explicitly portrayed as the good shepherd who lays down his life for the sheep (Jn. 10. 11–18; cf. Heb. 13. 20; 1 Pet. 2. 25). This metaphor which is applied to Christ is also used of one particular form of Christian ministry, and the same Greek word, *poimēn*, is translated 'pastors' in Eph. 4. 11, where pastors are grouped with four other types of ministry. While the noun is not used of ministers elsewhere in the New Testament its cognate verb is used twice. St. Paul bids the elders of Ephesus to act as shepherds to the Church, and St. Peter exhorts another group of elders to tend the flock of God which is their charge (Acts 20. 28; 1 Pet. 5. 2).

What are we to make of this image today? How are we to translate it? In the secular city there are neither sheep nor shepherds. Many people have never seen a sheep and few have seen a shepherd. In Africa sheep are seldom shepherded or folded; they run wild, as anyone who has driven along African roads knows well, and if they have a protector it is likely to be a small boy, very much a hireling whose own the sheep are not. This image then needs a reinterpretation which can come about only by a stripping and a rebirth, but to be effective this depends on the original picture being understood. For Jesus the shepherd stood for responsible leadership; he represented deep and selfless caring, a capacity for looking after others. If we translate this image for contemporary society we find that it can describe a surprisingly large range of people. The list would include teachers, doctors, managers, nurses, almoners, social workers, trade union officials, shop stewards, probation officers, psychiatric case-workers, club leaders, members of parliament, and many others. It is emphatically not an ecclesiastical preserve and it is not confined to the clergy. Whether they recognise it or not a vast number of people are in positions of responsibility for others, and this shepherd figure is held out before them by Jesus Christ as an ideal to imitate. In any civilised and progressive community the clergyman will be merely one of several functionaries with particular pastoral responsibility.

This lecture will concentrate chiefly on the role of the Christian pastor who happens to be ordained, but we shall not forget that his is a shared ministry and that many of those with whom he shares it have equal and sometimes greater pastoral responsibilities. I use the word pastor deliberately in the hope that it may be rehabilitated. In Anglican circles there has been a certain shyness about it, perhaps because it is associated with Baptists. In much of Africa, however, the clergy are known as pastors; Lutherans use it and so do Roman Catholics, as a glance at the index to the documents of Vatican II will verify. But Anglicans have never shunned the adjective 'pastoral' and even Oxford has a chair of moral and pastoral theology. What more could a word need to enhance its reputation for respectability?

Let us start with a quick succession of illustrations. These are drawn from my own travels and vivid recollections during the last twelve years or so. I need not bother you with dates for the situation has hardly changed. I remember once attending the ordination of a friend in the vast cathedral of St. John the Divine, New York. Fifteen young men were made deacons for service in one of the world's largest and least backward cities. Among the functions ascribed to their office by the Bishop reading the Ordinal was that they were to 'search for the sick, poor, and impotent people of the Parish, that they may be relieved with the alms of the

Parishioners or others'. That is a verbatim quotation from
the American Prayer Book in line with what is required at
the ordination of Anglican deacons in all cathedrals round
the world, and they vow to do this gladly and willingly. No
one showed any hesitation in assenting. Exactly the same
promise was made by one whose whole diaconate was to be
spent teaching in a theological seminary, and doubtless by
many others elsewhere whose life-long ministry may be
extra-parochial. With the exception of the limited number
of duties permitted to him in the church services, such as
reading Homilies and instructing the youth in the Cate-
chism, the Anglican deacon appears to have no other function. If it were only a matter of modernising a few words
and demythologising a few hallowed forms our task would
be relatively simple, for that is the least of our problems.
There are others.

At a clergy school in Nigeria where the subject was evangelism, one African pastor said with complete sincerity: 'I
am so busy raising money that I have no time to preach
Christ.' Some clergy would be less honest but their plight
would be the same. In Khartoum I once met a young
Sudanese pastor from the Nuba mountains who saw
another clergyman only once a year after making a journey
of 600 miles. In an anglo-catholic diocese in Tanzania a
missionary lamented to me: 'our priests can only say mass,
hear confessions and see that people die in a state of grace'.
In West Pakistan I talked one day with a pastor in whose
parish were a hundred and seventy village congregations in
his sole charge; he had one deacon and a handful of catechists to help him. In the Middle East I was entertained by
a priest who had just returned from two years in an American seminary where he had become an honorary citizen of
Texas. The result of this experience was that his main pre-
occupation had become the erection of as many shops and
garages as could be accommodated in his church compound. In South India a devoted presbyter remarked to
me: 'Yesterday thirteen starving Christians came to my
house to beg for food. They all had a testimony.' He gave
what he had, but it was little. Yet on another occasion an
American priest seriously recommended that I should treat
myself one night at a New York restaurant where dinner

for two would cost one hundred dollars. In contrast to this I recall with affection a priest in Ceylon who in a simple ashram near Kurunagala lives the Christian life in the framework of a Buddhist monk in utter simplicity and poverty. During a clergy conference in the diocese of Zulu-land, South Africa, where the great and belovéd Bishop Zulu is the only diocesan bishop in South Africa, a young white priest remarked to me that he had come into the diocese with all the usual prejudices against Africans, wondering how he could possibly work under an African bishop; but as he came to know his bishop, all his misgivings and prejudices quickly fell away. At another clergy conference in West Africa an angry young African priest, recently returned from England, came into the final session late, determined to spoil it by rattling the coins and keys in his trouser pockets to express resentment that the conductor was a European visitor, finally getting up to walk out noisily before the end and thus register his protest. I recount all this partly to give samples of the variety of clergy and partly to indicate that I have lost any illusions I may have had. There is no education to compare with travel, especially if you are able to live at the grass roots and move outside the big cities.

But there are two other pictures I would like to give, both from Uganda. The first is of a group of African pastors, led by their rural dean, visiting the cement works in a new industrial area. Seeing a factory and machinery and the speed and noise and tools of modern industry for the first time in their lives, their eyes and mouths opened wider and wider in a mixture of wonder, bewilderment, and dismay, for the sight and its meaning were beyond anything with which they were familiar or could easily comprehend. The second picture is of a gifted young African priest, who was in charge of a large church around which were two secondary schools and a teacher training college, providing a huge and fairly intelligent Sunday congregation. He was the only priest in the diocese sufficiently educated to minister effectively to a congregation of this type. But on Sundays as on many week-days he had to itinerate in the surrounding village churches of this extensive parish to provide simple, and often illiterate, villagers with the sacraments, while at

the central church both the preaching of the Word and the
taking of the services were left to a rather inadequate lay
reader whose qualifications would not have enabled him
even to enter the teacher training college, the standards of
which were in any case lower than that of either of the two
schools. This situation, which is typical and could still be
multiplied dozens of times all over Africa, shows something
of the anomaly in our Anglican theory and practice of
ministry. There is no lack of comparable conditions in other
churches.

I make no apology for asking you to consider the Christian ministry in Africa and Asia rather than Australia or
Britain, but if reasons are required I can give three. First,
the Churches in these continents really are facing a crisis
and one big part of that crisis concerns ministry. Second,
because these Churches have grown up during the last one
hundred and fifty years and outside western culture, the
problems are high-lighted and can be seen in themselves,
not so much confused by the stranglehold of tradition.
There is a sense in which younger churches are admirable
laboratories for studying New Testament problems of this
kind. Third, we live at a time when it is impossible to look
at churches in isolation from one another. None of us belongs primarily to a national church; we are part of a universal church. 'If one organ suffers, they all suffer together.
If one flourishes, they all rejoice together' (1 Cor. 12. 26). We
are not likely to solve our own problems if we ignore what
is happening in Chile, Jamaica, Rhodesia, Nigeria, and
Singapore. This is what mutual responsibility and interde-
pendence mean.

It is rather curious that although liturgical revision has
gone ahead with a large measure of support for new services of baptism and holy communion, and there are Anglican provinces in which the 1662 communion service is
almost unknown, nevertheless there has been far less pressure to revise the Ordinal. No doubt this is because it is less
frequently used, and its language is solemn and splendid
even if in places obscure and badly out of date. The classic
definition of Anglican priesthood is given by the bishop in
his exhortation to the candidates. Their calling is 'to be
messengers, watchmen, stewards of the Lord; to teach and

to premonish, to feed and provide for the Lord's family; to seek for Christ's sheep that are dispersed abroad ... that they may be saved through Christ for ever'. The emphasis is on two main aspects of ministry: that which is liturgical and performed inside the church, namely the ministry of Word and Sacrament, and that which is pastoral and to some extent performed outside the church as the minister moves among his people. Great stress is laid on the priest's spiritual responsibility, on the importance of his own example, and on the need for spiritual discipline. All this is good and few would want it changed.

But there are other points that call for attention. First, the definition of a priest's job presupposes Christendom; in seventeenth-century England we could hardly expect otherwise. This no longer exists in Europe and it has never existed anywhere else. The reference to seeking Christ's dispersed sheep would seem to refer to the lapsed rather than to the outsider or the pagan. Second, the present Ordinal assumes the parish system. When it was compiled the Church of England had little awareness of the heathen world beyond its own shores and no thought of a day when within its territorial bounds a majority of the population would either ignore or renounce the Christian faith; it had no missionary work at that time and no diocese beyond the British Isles. Yet the same Ordinal is still used not only in an England which it never envisaged but throughout the Anglican Communion in countries whose situation makes parts of it pitiably inappropriate. Imagine ordaining a man to the Anglican ministry in Persia, for example, where the total number of Anglicans hardly exceeds one thousand in a population of more than twenty million Muslims, or a primitive Indian in the Paraguyan Chaco or Southern Chile, or a young Japanese in Tokyo with its teeming eleven million inhabitants, and using an ordinal which assumes both Christendom and the parish system! A third point to observe is that its intention is to ordain men to a ministry which is primarily pastoral and certainly full-time. But there have always been those in Orders who have seldom or never engaged in a pastoral ministry, such as Fellows of Oxford and Cambridge Colleges, who, until the nineteenth-century reforms, could obtain their fellowships

in no other way. Apart from these there have been the
school-master parsons and the staffs of church societies, and
now there is a gradual development of part-time ministries,
exercised by men who are not going to be employed as the
Ordinal indicates. Fourth, although the Reformers drasti-
cally modified the notion of priesthood in their re-definition
of the Christian ministry, they still clung to the idea of a
professional class over against the rest of the Church. It is
true that the second Good Friday Collect prays for 'all
estates of men' in the Church, 'that every member of the
same, in his vocation and ministry' may serve God, but this
wider view of ministry, as belonging in some form to all the
people of God, does not emerge even by implication in the
Ordinal.

We are suggesting that the theory, the theology, of ministry in modern Anglicanism needs re-examination in the
light of the New Testament and that the Ordinal urgently
needs revision. But when we turn to things as they are we
find a very wide gap between theory and practice. This is
best illustrated by the situation in Africa. There is general
recognition that up till now Africa represents the most
striking success of the modern missionary movement. In
some respects this statement would need qualifying but in
terms of statistics the size of the total Christian community
in Africa has grown remarkably during the present century.
The total population of Africa south of the Sahara is estimated at 230 million, and the number of Christians 60
million (See T. A. Beetham, *Christianity and the New
Africa*, 1967, p. 22). Accurate figures are notoriously difficult to come by, but one fact is indisputable. In all
churches, Roman Catholic, Anglican, and Protestant, the
growth of the total Christian community has far outstrip-
ped the provision of ordained ministers to shepherd it. A
Roman Catholic theologian calls this 'the law of strangula-
tion' See Bengt Sundkler, *The Christian Ministry in Africa*,
1960, p. 81). Another Roman Catholic missionary scholar
has estimated the following ratios of priests to people in his
own Church throughout Africa. In 1966 there were 27
million catholics in all Africa and 15,000 priests, making a
ratio of 1 : 1,800. On present trends in 1980 the ratio would
be 1 : 2,400, and in the year 2000 1 : 3,500. (Adrian Hastings,

Church and Mission in Modern Africa, 1967, p. 212.) The gravity of this cannot be exaggerated. This shortage of clergy means that Christian communities cannot be adequately pastored and taught. Moreover, this is not a problem that can be alleviated by the recruitment of large numbers of missionary priests, for even if they were available it is doubtful if they would be admitted to many of these countries on a sufficient scale. The only answer is a rapid increase of indigenous clergy and an adjustment from western and medieval concepts of ministry to those which we find in the New Testament. Let us therefore look again at the five types or patterns of ministry which were considered at the end of the last lecture to see if they can provide any kind of answer to the present crisis.

First, there was the principle of differentiation and delegation, the refusal on the part of the apostles to be multifunctional. Second, there was the recognition that the gift of the Spirit in the community meant that every member of the people of God had some kind of ministry to perform. Third, there was the concept of ministry being a group activity at all levels; it was not individualistic or monarchical. Fourth, there were the distinctions between spheres of responsibility, and between those whose ministry was local and those whose calling was to travel and to be available to many congregations. Fifth, the idea of ministry being essentially voluntary and combined with secular callings was prior to the emergence of a professional and full-time class of ministers within the community; while in the nature of things such a development could not be avoided it was never intended to exclude or replace the original emphasis. A recovery of the *attitude* of ministry on the part of the whole Church in its relation to the world is necessary if the Lordship of Jesus Christ is to be interpreted today, and only such a recovery will bring with it a new understanding of what the various ministries within the Church should be and how they should operate.

Bishop F. R. Barry has suggested that we ought to begin, not with the question, what is a priest? but with the question, what is a layman? (F. R. Barry, *Vocation and Ministry,* 1958 p. xiii). The Christian Church was launched as a lay movement and 'the simple lay-character of the Apostles is

clearly evident' (H. Kraemer, *A Theology of the Laity*,
1958, p. 19). It is almost a truism these days to point out
that to be a layman simply means to be a Christian, a
member of the *laos* of God. In the early Church some of
these laymen were set aside to perform certain functions on
behalf of the others, functions which were to be taken over
by those subsequently to be called clergy, some of which
were restricted to them. We see the beginning of this with
the apostolic decision in Acts 6. But this decision was about
functions not status. The apostles were not making themselves a class apart, a separated caste such as the medieval
clergy were to become. The purpose was to achieve a corporate but differentiated ministry. Yet, as Leslie Paul has
shown, 'the relationship between clergy and laity has hardly
ever been since the first centuries that of a corporate ministry. The notion of two sorts of Christians, not simply
different in function but different in merit, in stature, in
authority, goes back at least to the legal formalism Christianity received from the Roman Empire. When the Christian laity of Europe in medieval times and subsequently
was "the world" ... to preach to the world was to preach to
the laity'. But this has all changed. 'The worshipping laity
is no longer coincident with "the world". The laity and the
ordained ministry are "over against" a world which by and
large does not accept either of them ... At the point where
the church discovers the common identity of the ministry
and the laity over against a world from which both are
separated, it discovers that *the laity works in that world*, has
its vocations there and is strategically placed for an historic
mission which the purely ministerial and hierarchical
church forgot for centuries. For these reasons the great debate is upon us. The laity has a ministry as real as that of
the ordained ministry: that ministry is to "the world", because that is where the laity *is*. Its ministry is only functionally separate from that of the ordained ministries: both
together constitute the corporate pastorate of the Body of
Christ in the world' (Leslie Paul, *The Deployment and Pay-
ment of the Clergy*, 1964, 149 f.). Bishop Barry puts the
same point with startling simplicity. 'The priest does not
cease to belong to the laity when he is ordained to the
priesthood—he is given a special commission and function

in it. The Ministry is the ministry of the whole Church and it is to be exercised by the whole Church' (op. cit., p. 41). This kind of approach may seem radical to traditionalists, but unlike some kinds of radicalism it belongs to the New Testament and is not alien to it.

The significance of the Acts 6 decision is that the apostles were clear that while all ministries had to be exercised by the Church, not all ministries had to be exercised by them. Their own primary concentration was to be on the ministry of the Word and prayer. Here were the first ingredients of full-time ministry. Neither sacramental nor administrative functions are mentioned, yet these would generally be assumed as the main ingredients of full-time ministers to-day. Ought this so to be? Infinitely more training and ability are required for those who are to minister the Word effectively than for the much simpler ministry of sacraments, and a good deal of administration could well be done by qualified members of the laity, as the apostles themselves saw in appointing the seven. But ministry is also related to prayer and the Ordinal stresses this. Addressing the candidates for priesthood the bishop hopes that 'as much as lieth in you, you will apply yourselves wholly to this one thing, and draw all your cares and studies this way; and that you will continually pray to God the Father ... for the heavenly assistance of the Holy Ghost'. Anglicans therefore expect of their clergy a spiritual ministry. They want them to be men who know God, who believe in him and can impart this faith convincingly and infectiously. As Leslie Paul wisely wrote, the nature of ministry 'forces upon it the self-effacing burden of communicating Another's word, Another's command, Another's love' (op. cit., 91 f.). Few are likely to disagree that in the life of the ordained nothing is more difficult than prayer and the ministry of the Word. But if this ministry is to be apostolic these priorities remain. They are two sides of the same coin, because the communication of God's Word is in the last analysis not a matter of the intellect alone but of spiritual understanding and receptivity which are cultivated more by prayer than by learning. If then we are to have an effective ministry *by* the people of God to the world, this can only come about as there is an effective ministry *to* the people of God by the ministers of the Word.

We may now turn to consider lay ministry. The fundamental lay ministry is to be a Christian, visibly and sometimes audibly, in the secular world. This *is* ministry. It is
expressed in the way a man does his job, the way a woman
runs her home; it is expressed in relationships of care, in a
concern for persons beyond the ordinary, in the willingness
to go the second mile; it is also expressed in voluntary service of one kind or another additional to the work which
provides one's living. Such voluntary service will not necessarily be church work or even under the auspices of the
church. Often it may be in co-operation with people outside
the Church, and this will be good for it provides natural
opportunities for witness and dialogue. It was with this in
view that Harry Daniel, a presbyter of the Church of South
India, encouraged the cathedral congregation at Bangalore
to involve themselves in certain social activities with both
Hindus and Muslims. Men and women who are struggling
in various organisations such as the United Nations to
bring about peace or prevent war, those who are seeking to
establish justice, to conquer disease, to banish poverty and
hunger, are all exercising ministries which are quite as
authentic as anything the clergy attempt and often much
more onerous. This is the kind of ministry that thousands
of Christians are offering to God and through him to the
world, for Christian ministry is a great deal more than the
taking of services in church and the visiting of church
members in their homes, and what the clergy do is but a
fragment of the total ministry of the people of God. There
is constant need for the reminder that 'the laity are not the
helpers of the clergy so that the clergy can do their job, but
the clergy are helpers of the whole people of God, so that
the laity can be the Church' (Hans-Ruedi Weber, quoted by
J. A. T. Robinson, *The New Reformation*, 1965, p. 55).

There are of course simpler and more everyday forms of
lay ministry which are innumerable. The work of the dis-
trict nurse, the midwife, the youth who visits a lonely old
woman, the man who has a kind and cheerful word, the
woman who makes cups of tea for the weary, the volunteer
typists and messengers who make communication possible
—all these and many more are exercising a real and neces-

sary ministry deserving far more recognition than such service is usually given. The special responsibility of the clergy is to enable every Christian for whom they have pastoral care to find some form of active ministry, however humble, to see their daily work in terms of ministry and witness, and by encouragement to keep them up to the mark. It is through such deeds of love and acts of witness that they discover the Holy Spirit and his gifts.

The third point that emerged in our New Testament study was the corporate nature of ministry, the need for a combination of various gifts, various ministries, if the Church in any one place is to exist in fulness and to make its full impact on society. Christ's gifts to his Church were 'some to be apostles, some prophets, some evangelists, some pastors and teachers' (Eph. 4. 11). How is this to be understood today and what are the modern equivalents? An important suggestion has been made by John Taylor which I propose to summarise here. Apostles may be seen as those whose chief function is *episkopé* for mission. This oversight is concerned principally with the Gospel and only by derivation with the Church. They are charged with guarding the *kerygma*, leading the team, co-ordinating the ministries of others. Prophets are those who receive particular insight and inspiration, who are prepared to go against the tide, to challenge public opinion, to fight on behalf of man's humanity amid the structures of technopolis, to join in the struggle for civil rights and racial equality. Men like Martin Luther King are obvious examples of such contemporary prophets but a majority of them may well be laymen. Evangelists are those committed to presenting the Gospel to people who have not heard it or who have rejected it. Today they will often be engaged in dialogue with Marxists or Humanists or those of other faiths. At times their role will be that of the apologist, but they will also be seeking contact with the fringers and outsiders. Teachers may well be seen as theologians, not just the creative thinkers and writers, but also those who interpret their message for the wayfaring man who may not have time or education for reading them in the original. In some situations they will be on call as resource personnel when a discussion group reaches a point where it needs someone with expert knowledge of the Bible or of some doctrinal question. An increasing number of theologians today are lay people as they have been for generations in the Greek Orthodox Church. Finally there are the pastors. As we saw at the beginning of this lecture the pastoral role is fulfilled by a large variety of people today in many different jobs, but if we want one word to describe in modern terms this particular ministry it would surely be counselling. Social work, psychiatric practice, clinical theology, the ministry of healing and consolation and encouragement, all combine in shaping the Church's pastoral ministry today and among pastors there will be many sub-divisions of specialisation and expertise. (For a fuller discussion see John V. Taylor, *Change of Address*, 1968, chapter 12, especially pp. 149 ff.)

If the early Church needed to see ministry in a great variety of persons and functions all co-operating, how much more is this necessary in the much more complex society of the second half of the twentieth century? Renaissance man who could claim a reasonably complete acquaintance with all that could be known has gone for ever. In every sphere specialisation has been forced upon us by the sheer advance of knowledge on an unprecedented scale. It is claimed, for example, that of all the scientists who have ever lived 90 per cent are alive today, and 'at one of the recent international congresses for atomic research, it was established that it would take a scientist his whole life just to read the reports and documentation of this one congress' (quoted in *Study Encounter*, Vol. III, No. 3, p. 111). In such a world we cannot hope to provide a relevant ministry if this is seen in terms of the monarchical parson, holding some parish fort single-handed, expected to take services, preach helpfully, provide marriage guidance, run a youth club, manage a plant of some size, raise money, visit several hundred homes regularly, and present the Gospel to the rank outsider. This is not one man's job and it should never have been so regarded. The answer is not, I think, the abolition of the parish system as such but, at least in some areas, both rural and urban, its re-organisation into larger units. It is obviously impossible for parishes as they are today to have a team of ministers who between them have all the gifts we have just reviewed. But there has been sufficient experimenting in group ministries to prove that a much more varied distribution of gifts can be made available when a small-sized town is taken as a unit or when several inner-city or village churches combine into one group. Such groupings should never be arbitrarily drawn up. In the initial stages even at best they are not easy to work, but they never work unless full account is taken of geographical and sociological factors, and field research may be a necessary preliminary. At one and the same time group ministries may help to meet the problems of clerical loneliness and the congregations who suffer undeservedly from one man's limitations.

The fourth feature we noticed in the New Testament and early Church was the distinction between local and itinerant ministry, and also that between spontaneous and authorised (or ordained) ministry. The speed of modern transport makes itinerant ministries possible today on a scale previously undreamed of. Even the Pope travels internationally. Prophets, evangelists, teachers, can be increasingly at the service of the whole Church. As the doors of some countries close to professional missionaries on a long-term basis it is well to remember that many of them are open to short-term visitors. There are situations where one such visitor or a small team can make a very great contribution by leading or assisting in clergy and lay training conferences, training about stewardship or group life, industrialisation and urbanisation, seminars on other faiths and current problems, retreats, and, where the opportunity exists, even missions. Specialised ministries of a mobile kind should be developed; some forms of this, possibly in ecumenical and international teams, might well become the successor to the traditional ex-patriate missionary where he is no longer welcome. The permanence of mission is not tied to the permanence of the missionary or a particular vintage of missionary, good though that vintage may be! Our second distinction suggests that far more attention should be paid to spontaneous and unordained ministries than has been customary. Very often these are charismatic, sometimes unconventional to an embarrassing degree. The historic churches with a strong sense of order have not been noted either for their emphasis on the Holy Spirit or their

welcome to any novel manifestations of his energy. This
inadequate recognition of the Pentecostal element which
runs through the whole Christian faith and Gospel
accounts, more than any other single factor, for the un-
parallelled growth of Pentecostalism in a nominally Roman
Catholic South America and also for the emergence
throughout Africa of approximately six thousand independent Churches which have broken away from both Catholic
and more often Protestant churches with about seven million adherents (David B. Barrett, *Schism and Renewal in
Africa*, Nairobi, 1968, p. 3). Room must be made for the
spontaneous and the unprogrammed, the unstructured and
the breaks with tradition, if ministry today is to bear a
more complete resemblance to ministry in the first Christian era. As one consultant remarked at the last Lambeth
Conference, 'the New Testament does not encourage Christians to think that nothing should be done for the first
time'.

Finally, we have to notice what Roland Allen called 'the
Case for Voluntary Clergy', the only kind there were in the
early centuries. It would be foolish and unrealistic to state
this in such a way as to suggest that the very idea of professional clergy was a mistake. Inevitably the Church became institutionalised, for this is the only way communities
survive in history, and therefore it needed full-time officials.
On this there can be no going back. Our present difficulties
arise from taking this as the norm and showing a reluctance
to accept any kind of supplementary clergy. It is useless to
suppose that the recovery of the permanent diaconate is a
sufficient answer. The point of pressure is the administration of the sacraments, and in the Anglican Church this
necessitates priests. The provision of the weekly Eucharist
for every Christian congregation is far more urgent than an
intensive theological education of those ordained to cele-
brate the Eucharist. Unlike Lutherans and Presbyterians,
Anglicans have been nothing like so particular about the
training they give to those permitted to minister the Word,
for which much more knowledge and skill are desirable.
(For Roman Catholic support of this view see Adrian Hastings, *Church and Mission in Modern Africa*, p. 232.) St.
Paul ordained local elders, men of good character and

standing, to exercise a ministry of leadership which undoubtedly would have included presiding at the Lord's
Supper. For the most part we are so imprisoned in our
tradition that we are frightened to do this, notwithstanding
resolutions of successive Lambeth Conferences. Of course
there are risks, but they are no greater than in allowing a
vast assortment of sparsely trained men to preach and
teach, which is the practice in most of Africa and much of
Asia.

Two kinds of voluntary clergy might be envisaged. First,
there would be those who already have professional qualifications and are in positions of responsibility in the secular
world. Some in this category have been ordained in South
India, Hong Kong, and elsewhere. They would continue in
their secular jobs but by virtue of ordination be able to
exercise a sacramental ministry as well as doing what lay
readers do at present. It is this kind of person who is particularly needed in the West. The second category would be
quite different, resembling rather the Pentecostal pastors in
Brazil and Chile. Their qualifications would not be intellectual but those of character as set out in the pastoral
epistles. In African villages they would do the work the
catechist does now. Unlike the catechist, however, they
would not fall between two stools. The catechist lacks the
authority and education of the clergy, but neither does he
have the independence and value of a real layman because
he is employed in the full-time service of the Church.
Catechists have been heroic figures in the past—many of
them still are—but today there is something almost tragic
in their role. Their replacement by ordained ministers is a
matter of urgency. None of these voluntary clergy would be
in positions of sole charge, whichever category they belong
to. Their ministry would have to be supplementary, in the
one case through lack of time, in the other through lack of
training, for the very conditions and limitations of this kind
of ministry would demand the leadership of someone fully
trained who could weld such colleagues into a team and
guide them responsibly. The need for these part-time ministries will always be greater in rapidly growing churches. In
more settled and established churches the needs are not so
great but the benefits could be considerable. The only

criterion is that each Christian community should be adequately pastored. In some parts of the Anglican Communion this stage has been reached, but in many it has
not.

Finally, there are two points at which confusion must at
all costs be avoided. First, let it be clear that voluntary
ministry is for the benefit of the Church, not the world.
This is its main difference from the worker-priest movement. Nothing must obscure the pre-eminent role of the
laity, qua laity, in the secular world. No one *needs* to be
ordained—whether as priest or deacon—in order to give
witness in daily life and work, as Miss Mollie Batten reminded the 1968 Lambeth Conference in memorable words.
Ministry belongs to *all* Christian people and is directed
towards the world. Ordained ministry is a calling to *some*
Christian people and is directed chiefly towards the Church.

Secondly, there is a good deal of concern in some circles,
not least in Africa but also in the West, about the changing
status of the clergy. It has varied through the centuries,
being determined both by the standing of Christianity in a
particular society, and also by the social and educational
standards of clergy in comparison with other members of
the community. In Africa, for example, the status of the
pastor was artificially high when in the early days of the
modern missionary movement he was one of the few people
who could read. Now it has declined sharply because the
education of the clergy has seldom kept pace with that of
many others in their congregations and, as is sometimes
said, the pew is higher than the pulpit. It is silly to pretend
that status does not matter, for it affects the job and the
way the job is done. Nevertheless, the aim of this lecture
has been to suggest that function should be our prior concern. Once we are clear about function, status can look after
itself. Status is relative, not fixed; to a great extent it depends on function. Nowhere these days can the clergy take
status for granted and assume a particular rank; this is to
look ridiculous. In secular society status has to be earned
and won. In few places can the clergy speak with authority
because they are clergy and expect that authority to be
recognised. In today's world the only authority that counts
is the authority of competence and the authority of

character. Translated into biblical terms this means knowledge and holiness. In so far as the clergy make the grade in these two spheres they have little to fear for their future, but without these no status has worth and no ministry can be assured of effect.

IV. THE GOSPEL AND OTHER FAITHS

ONE of the new features of the modern world is the changing geography of religion. This has greatly accelerated since the end of World War II and has important bearing on the study of Christian mission and ministry. Until well into this century it would have been an infrequent experience for Europeans to meet people of another faith unless they travelled in Asia and Africa. With the exception of a few academics and the more intelligent missionaries little attention was paid to the content of these other faiths, even by Christians. Today the situation is very different and for a Christian to be ignorant about other religions is a serious handicap. The chief reason for this is that we now live increasingly in a multi-religious society, the inevitable corollary of a multi-racial society. Two factors have brought this about: immigration and the missionary resurgence of the world's religions.

Migration is almost as old as man. Peoples have always moved, sometimes in search of food as when Israel went down into Egypt, sometimes in search of freedom as when the Pilgrim Fathers left Plymouth for New England. Often overcrowding or the promise of better economic conditions or indented labour have led to migration. This largely accounts for the Chinese diaspora throughout South East Asia, the presence of Indians in great numbers throughout Africa as well as in places as far apart as Malaya, Fiji, and Trinidad, and for the considerable numbers of Japanese in Brazil. One religious result of this is that in many cities of the world there are churches, mosques, temples, and pagodas. Even Honolulu, the playground of American millionaires, exemplifies this. The new factor in Britain is that whereas in the past the people of our islands themselves migrated to colonise or build empires, taking their religion with them, now the movement is in reverse and we are at the receiving end for the first time of migrant communities on a large scale. The majority of these are of a different race and colour. While those from the Caribbean are usually Christians, those from India and Pakistan are more often of a different religion, particularly Hindus, Sikhs, and Muslims. In England the transport service and some industries would find survival difficult if not impossible without them, and in the Health Service 41 per cent of hospital doctors come from overseas. Thousands of students, chiefly from Africa and Asia, enter the universities of Europe, North America, and Australia every year, adding not only to their international character but also making them multi-religious. Thus, in universities and in many of our towns and cities we already have a condition of inter-religion.

But the change is not merely one of geographical redis-tribution brought about by movements of population. It is also the result of revival and renewal in religions which many nineteenth-century missionaries thought would rapidly decline and soon altogether disappear. This was their prayer and hope and faith. History shows them to have been mistaken, but for this they cannot be blamed. In the first place the initial encounter of Europeans and Americans—quite apart from missionaries—with these other religions was generally in their most debased form. Those who went to India could be awe-struck by its archi-tectural splendours, its literature and culture, but equally horrified by many of the features of popular Hinduism. Secondly, it was relatively easy for our forefathers in the last century to assume the superiority of Christianity be-cause of its link with both civilisation and imperial power. For them it was unthinkable that all resistance should not finally break down before their offers of what was held to be so much better politically, culturally, and religiously. Owen Chadwick has written: 'The Victorians changed the face of the world because they were assured. Untroubled by doubt whether Europe's civilisation and politics were suited to Africa or Asia, they saw vast opportunities open to energy and enterprise, and identified progress with the spread of English intelligence and English industry' (Owen Chad-wick, *The Victorian Church*, Vol. 1, 1966, p. 1). Thirdly, of all the religions at that time Christianity alone displayed missionary zeal. Originally it had moved ever further westward starting from the east, but from the middle of the eighteenth century in an unprecedented manner it began to move ever further eastward starting from the west. Until then religions had been mostly regional. The sixteenth-century formula *cujus regio, ejus religio* obtained generally. Islam was to be found in North Africa, the Middle East, parts of India, Malaya, Indonesia. Buddhism predominated in S.E. Asia, China, and Japan. Hinduism was strictly Indian and for Indians. These religions had no westward outreach and no desire to convert westerners. They were not at that time missionary religions; they showed signs of decadence.

This is no longer the case. The renewal in each has been very much a missionary renewal. Furthermore, since the coming of independence to the countries of Asia and the Middle East the ancient ethnic religions have come to play an important cultural role, providing a moral fabric and spiritual base for the life of the people as Christianity had done for their former conquerors. Thus Arab nationalism is very closely associated with Islam to countercheck the Zionism which is one aspect of Israel and the Christianity which is one aspect of Europe and North America. In India, the militant Hindu party with its swastika symbol, one of whose members assassinated Mahatma Gandhi, is gaining ground every week. Its vision is of an India in which Christians and Muslims will find no place. Its political wing is the Jan Sangh Party, its cultural wing the Hindu Mahasaba with its campaign motto 'Save India from Christian imperialism'. Buddhism has filled much the same role in the life of Burma and Ceylon in the years since independence.

But I would invite you to look at the missionary renewal of the great religions and I select four examples. First let me say that on travels in India I myself have been at the receiving end of Hindu evangelism a number of times. I say evangelism and not propaganda, for those who spoke to me were convinced that Hinduism possessed an infinitely greater wealth and conferred a far more wonderful benefit than Christianity. They were not fanatics. They were bear-

THE GOSPEL AND OTHER FAITHS

ing their own testimony to their own faith. I have met this at both ends of Hinduism, in the widely open Ramakrishna Movement with its willingness to absorb all that is worthy in any religion, and in the rigid and anti-European Arya Samaj which is fiercely Hindu. Christopher Isherwood's novel *Meeting by the River* is about two English brothers, one of whom becomes a Hindu monk. It is not based on fancy. My second example comes from Japan, a land of 100 million people, in which a number of new and syncretistic religions flourish in a remarkable way. The most powerful of these is Soka Gakkai, the fastest growing religion in the world. It claims no fewer than $6\frac{1}{2}$ million families, about 20 million people in all, one-fifth of Japan's population. The claim may be exaggerated but not all that much. It was founded only in 1930. After World War II its numbers were in thousands not millions. Its name means 'Creative-Value Study Society.' Its political or secular arm is Komeito or 'clean government party', now one of the most powerful and popular political parties in Japan. The point to notice about this religion is not so much what it believes but the astonishing speed of its growth in less than twenty years.

My third example must be from Islam, self-consciously propagating itself as never before, through Radio Mecca's Voice of Islam, the Al Azhar centre in Cairo preparing a special core of missionaries and instructors, and above all the active and willing witness of hundreds of thousands of simple Muslims. Islam is expanding spontaneously in Africa today. In one recent year it claimed 9 million new African converts. Its heterodox Ahmadiyya sect has a highly structured missionary organisation with headquarters in West Pakistan and institutes in many parts of Africa. It makes an explicit attack on Jesus Christ; it has considerable numerical success, and of its converts in Ghana whereas one-third had previously been animists, two-thirds had been Christians. Africa's total Muslim population doubled between 1940 and 1960, and the figures for World Islam are approximately those of the Roman Catholic Church, some 450 million. There is a trickle of European converts to Islam, and the mosque at Woking claims an average of two converts a week. In Fiji I was taken to a young and thriving Muslim community which had grown from nothing in less than six years.

A fourth illustration of renewal for mission in another faith may be seen in Buddhism. Like Islam it can claim some notable western converts and apologists. It has study centres in many western cities. Perhaps another personal recollection will serve to make this point. In 1967 I had to attend a conference in Ceylon which lasted the inside of a week. I noticed every day that the national press was paying considerable attention to the departure of a Buddhist abbot at the end of that week for Ghana. He was going there as a Buddhist missionary, invited personally by Ceylon's High Commissioner in Accra, the first Buddhist missionary on African soil. According to the reports of the great motorcade which hailed his departure he took with him three things: a casket of relics, a statue of the Buddha, and a bo-sapling—it was under the bo tree that Gautama received his enlightenment. The very idea of a Buddhist mission in Africa is the chief significance of the incident.

The result of all this is our present situation of religious pluralism. In a way that has never been the case before all religions are in circulation and they are available to be seen in our own land and cities. Religious pluralism is not new to Asia; it is new to the West. If it leads to confusion here, how much more is this the case for Africans! It is reported that a social worker in Nigeria visited a youth in a back street of Lagos. On his bedside table he found the following books: the Bible, the Book of Common Prayer, the Quran, three copies of *Watchtower* (the magazine of Jehovah's Witnesses), a biography of Karl Marx, a book of Yoga exercises, and *How to Stop Worrying*. I can recall a fascinating visit to a Muslim family in Omdurman on the banks of the Nile opposite Khartoum. The father was a devout Muslim who had built a little prayer room in his compound where people from the dusty street might come and pray at the appointed hours. He had five sons. One had been in Eastern Europe and was now a Marxist; another had been in England and returned an agnostic; a third had embraced Buddhism. The fourth and fifth were still Muslims.

I have tried to set out some typical features of the contemporary scene. We must now turn to some of the problems that are thrown up and consider various attitudes that Christians have taken or are taking to other faiths. One problem pressing on churches in many British cities just now is whether they should seek to evangelise the Muslims, Sikhs, and Hindus who form substantial minorities of these urban populations. We send missionaries to Muslim countries such as Persia and Pakistan; what do we do about Muslims from these countries who settle and work in ours? Bradford, for example, has a community of at least 13,000 Muslims (the figure for 1966). Should the Church ignore them in the sense of letting them be and co-exist, or by active evangelism lay itself open to the charge of taking unfair advantage of their presence among us, or should it seek some course in between? This is an urgent missionary issue and like most questions the answer depends on one's theological position.

Three broadly different attitudes have been taken: the first may be called the conservative or rigid, the second liberal, and the third is middle-way or moderate. And there are variations and modifications within each.

The rigid view with a great deal of Christian tradition behind it, both Catholic and Protestant, regards Christianity as the one true religion, the outcome of unique revelation, and the other religions are dismissed as false, deceptive, and worthless, some would say inventions of the devil. It is hardly surprising that many of the nineteenth-century missionaries held this view somewhat crudely because of the culture shock arising from their experiences of the superstition, cruelty, and immorality of other religions. 'The Hinduism of Mahatma Gandhi and of Dr. Radhakrishnan is wondrously different from that which dismayed Henry Martyn so sorely in 1800' (K. Cragg, *Christianity in World Perspective*, 1968, p. 67). If our contemporaries were confronted by the things which were met by the early missionaries to India, notably infanticide and sati (suttee), the burning alive of the Hindu widow with the corpse of her husband, or by the powers of evil and witchcraft which can still be felt in many an African village, they would perhaps find themselves rather less liberal and sophisticated than they supposed. The conventional tourist in Africa and Asia does not spend weeks living in villages. Some of us

have. And those who do not believe in the devil in Europe
may have second thoughts if they stayed for a period in
areas that have never known the name of Christ. This view
therefore no more deserves to be lightly dismissed than un-
critically accepted. Nevertheless, when all this is allowed
for, the fact remains that at their best, the great religions of
mankind have produced good and holy men. If we are to
accept the criterion of Jesus, 'by their fruits you shall know
them', they cannot be written off as totally false and evil. In
one year not long ago the praesidium of the United Nations
consisted of a Buddhist, a Muslim, and a Hindu. Although
Gandhi loved the New Testament he drew chiefly on the
spiritual resources of his own Hindu literature, and no-one
who has listened to U Thant or read his speeches can scorn
the religion that nurtured him. Moreover, on this theory
millions and millions of our fellow human beings are con-
demned to annihilation or worse. Can we believe this and at
the same time believe in the God and Father of our Lord
Jesus Christ?

This negative view of other faiths has been held in a
more refined manner by such outstanding theologians as
Karl Barth and Hendrik Kraemer. Barth's celebrated assertion 'Religion is unbelief' was modified by Kraemer, but
with Barth he denied any continuity between other forms
of religion and the Christian Gospel. The Gospel is something utterly new, a complete break with anything previously known; all other religion is man's attempt to justify
himself and is to that extent victim of demonic powers.
Yet Kraemer was ready to recognise the reality of religious
experience outside the Christian revelation. He did not dis-
miss the quest for points of contact, and he preferred even
non-Christian religions to a closed secularism (see Carl F.
Hallencreutz, *Kraemer Towards Tambaram*, Uppsala, 1966,
especially pp. 298 ff.). But Kraemer did not believe that the
non-Christian religions were means of salvation in any
sense; his attitude was uncompromising and missionary.
Therefore he belongs essentially to the conservative wing
and is probably its best and most moderate spokesman.

The second attitude is the opposite, for it seeks to recognise and welcome truth in all religions and sees them as
ultimately leading to God. This approach and those who

take it have always been popular in India, especially among Hindus with their capacity for absorbing whatever they find attractive in other faiths. I remember once meeting a young Indian planter on an air journey. He told me that in his house he had a prayer room with a Hindu altar, a picture of Jesus, and a copy of the Quran. This respect for any religion with spirituality is typical of the Indian tradition which at its purest has no desire to be exclusive but on the contrary wants to include the best in all. In America many Christian leaders have adopted views approximating to this, and it reached its high peak of popularity in 1928 when it influenced the great Missionary Conference at Jerusalem. Christianity was presented by J. N. Farquhar as the Crown of Hinduism, and by others as the fulfilment of man's highest religious aspirations, and instead of the Old Testament providing a unique preparation for Christ, parallel preparation was found in other faiths.

This outlook still has a wide appeal because of its tolerance and openness and it can claim the support of some great names. Arnold Toynbee, while revering Christianity, held that all the higher religions were the same in essence. Their differences are the result of history; their unity is to be seen in the idea of self-renunciation and the awareness of a spiritual Presence beyond man. Paul Tillich insisted that Christianity was based on a revelatory event, the Christ-event, which has critical and transforming power for all religions. But Christ also judges Christianity and he can judge it through non-Christian religions, as for example through Islam, 'in its wisdom in dealing with the primitive peoples and in its solution of the racial problem' (P. Tillich, *Christianity and the Encounter of World Religions*, 1963, p. 87). In passing one might note that this is hardly evident in the Sudan. Because of this, according to Tillich, Christianity will no longer attempt to convert in the traditional and depreciated sense of this word, but will continue a dialogue which has already begun (ibid., p. 94 f.). More recently John Macquarrie has urged that 'the time has come for Christianity and the other great world religions to think in terms of sharing a mission to the loveless and unloved masses of humanity, rather than in sending missionaries to convert each other'. He calls this a global ecumenism. He believes that 'the time has come for an end to the kind of mission that proselytises, especially from sister faiths which, though under different symbols, are responding to the same God and realising the same quality of life'. He distinguishes between animistic cults and the 'higher' religions, and thinks that the Christian missionary should not aim at converting adherents of these latter 'in which God's saving grace is already recognisably at work' (John Macquarrie, *Principles of Christian Theology*, London, 1966, pp. 393–5). All this amounts to a religious relativism which fits in happily with the present climate of thought in many respects.

At the same time it elicits certain criticisms. In the first place, if the original Christians had thought like this there would have been no New Testament as we know it, no Church, no mission, and no universal Christianity today. Secondly, because of its relativism it does not take seriously the question of truth, to which genuine religion can never be indifferent. Thirdly, it leaves out of account the enormous differences between the contrasting characters of Jesus and Muhammad, between the theism of Christianity and Judaism and Islam, the atheism of many Buddhists, and the choice between polytheism, monism, and theism open to Hindus. Above all it obscures the immense difference between the Christian Gospel, which sees salvation, eternal life, peace, reconciliation, forgiveness, as gifts of God which we must humbly receive by faith, and most other religions which teach that these have to be worked for, struggled for, earned and deserved, perhaps even through a series of existences, human and animal.

A Roman Catholic variation of the liberal view will be found in Raymond Panikkar's important and popular book *The Unknown Christ of Hinduism* (London, 1965), which follows up the thesis proposed by Farquhar that Christ is the fulfilment of Hinduism, for Hinduism culminates in Christianity. In a penetrating critique Lesslie Newbigin notices that it is echoed in the Papal Encyclical *Suam Ecclesiam*. 'The picture given in this document is that of the religions as concentric circles grouped around a centre which is occupied by the Roman Catholic Church. Around this centre is a circle composed of other Christians. Beyond this lie other theists, adherents of pagan religions, and finally, at the outer periphery, those who profess no religion at all.' But Newbigin rightly protests that this model will not do. 'The other religions are not to be understood and measured by their proximity to or remoteness from Christianity. They are not beginnings which are completed in the Gospel ... To fit them into this model is to lose any possibility of understanding them. Moreover, what do the concepts of "near" and "far" mean in relation to the crucified and risen Jesus? Is the devout Pharisee nearer or further than the semi-pagan prostitute? Is the passionate Marxist nearer or further than the Hindu mystic? Is a man nearer to Christ because he is religious? Is the Gospel the culmination of religion or is it the end of religion?' (Lesslie Newbigin, *The Finality of Christ*, London, 1969, p. 43 f.). Kraemer had also criticised thirty years earlier what he regarded as a misuse of the fulfilment concept. 'Fulfilment is not the term by which to characterise the relation of the revelation in Christ to the non-Christian religions. To use it engenders inevitably the erroneous conception that the lines of the so-called highest developments point naturally in the direction of Christ, and would end in him if produced further. The Cross and its real meaning—reconciliation as God's initiative and act—is antagonistic to all human religious aspirations and ends, for the tendency of all human religious striving is to possess or conquer God, to realise our divine nature (theosis). Christ is not the fulfilment of this but the uncovering of its self-assertive nature; and at the same time the re-birth to a completely opposite condition, namely, the fellowship of reconciliation with God' (H. Kraemer, *The Christian Message in a Non-Christian World*, 1938, p. 123). And it needs to be remembered that when God's truth and holiness were made visible in Christ he was rejected, not by the irreligious but by the most moral, spiritual, and advanced religion of them all.

The student of religions or the prospective missionary might well feel confused in the light of all this. Is there no choice between these two extremes, no middle passage? There are signs that a moderate view is emerging both in Roman Catholic theology and also in the writings of some Anglican scholars of whom Kenneth Cragg is the most distinguished in this field. On the one hand it clearly affirms

that Jesus Christ is unique and divine; there has been no
one else like him. On the other hand it gives a positive
value to other religions, believing that God's Spirit has
always been at work in the cultures and faiths of men. In
themselves these faiths are not evil, for they have brought
help and hope to millions of people and have produced men
of wisdom and goodness. While most of those who take this
view would not regard other religions as offering revelation
and truth equal to that found in the Christian Scriptures
and in Jesus Christ, they would affirm that the world is a
better place because of the teachings of men like the
Buddha, Confucius, and Muhammad, which have lifted
countless generations of people from superstition and
idolatry to a higher and more moral way of life.

This more moderate position gets rid of some problems
but confronts us with others which do no arise in the same
way for those taking either of the extreme views. There are
two particularly haunting questions that have to be
examined. First, is salvation available to men of other
faiths? Second, should Christians seek to convert them to
Christ? A discussion about dialogue with men of other
faiths must wait till the next lecture.

It is not easy to approach the first of these questions dis-
passionately without either emotion or bias. Another way
of phrasing it, often used by Roman Catholics, asks, Is there
salvation outside the Church? Others enquire, What happens to pagans? This is an acute problem for Christians
because of their belief in God and in a future life. It does
not arise for atheists or for those who believe that death is
the end of existence. In general the Christian attitude has
undergone a seachange. Although some of the early
Fathers thought that good pagans would be saved, and in
Latin theology there grew up the notion of *Limbo*, and
Dante's Virgil was not in hell, nevertheless St. Augustine's
theology for the most part prevailed to inspire the missionaries of the middle ages and since. Men like St. Francis
Xavier accepted the rigours and dangers of long journeys
and missionary work because they were convinced that
those whom they did not baptise would be damned. Until
modern times this has continued to be a most powerful
missionary motive. The change that is now upon us is not

in the first instance the result of a different theology but rather the result of a different perspective and larger horizons. Hans Küng is one of those who has drawn attention to the enormous size numerically of non-Christian humanity. This is appreciated today in a way that was impossible even a hundred years ago. First, non-Christian history has been hugely prolonged backwards. Christ came 2,000 years ago but humanity may be 600,000 years or some millions of years in age. In comparison the history of the people of God is a small fraction of that time. He asks—at a conservative estimate—'Were all the people in the remaining round 590,000 years damned? And if not, how are they supposed to have been saved?' Secondly, the non-Christian world has been enormously enlarged in terms of space. In the Bible the world that could be envisaged was limited to the Mediterranean area and adjoining territories. The Americas, most of Africa, Asiatic Russia, the plains of India and China, the Pacific islands, were unknown, but countless millions had lived there for thousands of years before anyone preached Christ to them. Some of these peoples, like those in Uganda for example, were discovered for the first time less than one hundred years ago. And even now the numbers of non-Christians in Asia are multiplying at a rapid speed and most of them are beyond the reach of the Church. 'Are all these millions to be damned? And if not, how are they to be saved?' And thirdly, the non-Christian world has now thrust its way deep into the Christian world, and there is neo-paganism in the midst of what was once the Christian West. But many of these are not wicked people, and it is not their fault that they are pagans. So the question presses home: what happens to them? (Hans Küng, *That the World may Believe*, 1963, pp. 73–8.)

Turning to the New Testament we find a God whose love is immeasurable and inexhaustible and who is made known in Jesus Christ. If Jesus could pray for the forgiveness of those who crucified him, it is out of character with all that he stood for to think that his Father would not save in some way the millions who through no fault of their own had never heard of him. The New Testament is explicit on this point. 'God our Saviour ... desires all men to be saved and to come to the knowledge of the truth' (1 Tim. 2. 3, 4).

Here is a definition of the divine will beyond all doubt. To
believe that the eternal destiny of unnumbered millions is
contingent on the obedience of a minority of Christians
would expose God to a charge of the most monstrous
immorality and cruelty. With or without the Church he
wants all his children to reach the destiny he chose for
them. To imagine the masses being damned because of
ignorance and their lack of any opportunity for faith and
baptism is quite intolerable for most Christians today.

On the whole it is Roman Catholic scholars who have led
the way in wrestling with this problem. This is partly because their own doctrinal formularies are so profoundly
challenged by these new perspectives. There is a growing
consensus which would probably support two propositions.
First, it would be wrong to conclude that only Christians
can or will be saved. Second, it would be wrong to say that
men can be saved through Buddha or Muhammad or anyone else except Jesus Christ, for these others were teachers
not saviours. The long-held belief that there is no salvation
outside the Church—*extra ecclesiam nulla salus*—is gradually being abandoned. This theory was originally based on
St. Peter's image of the Church as the ark of salvation (1
Pet. 3. 20), but theologians are realising that too much has
been built upon it. The Fathers of the Church drew a negative inference from it, that those outside the ark could not
be saved, reading more into Peter's positive statement than
it can properly bear. Vatican II has modified this rigid
doctrine and affirmed that the grace of Christ can operate
outside the Church and that even those without explicit
knowledge of God may be saved (*Dogmatic Constitution on
the Church*, 2. 16). St. Paul seems to be implying this in
Romans 2. 11–16. It is even suggested that non-Christian
religions may have a positive role in so far as they express
genuine aspirations of their people to worship God, and
that though they may be far from God, God is not far from
them. Hans Küng speaks of them as providing *ordinary*
means of salvation in contrast to the *extraordinary* means
of salvation offered by the Church and its Gospel, for God
does sanction the religions as such as social structures. 'A
man is to be saved within the religion that is made available to him in his historical situation. Hence it is his right

and duty to seek God within that religion in which the hidden God has already found him. All this until such time as he is confronted in an existential way with the revelation of Jesus Christ' (Joseph Neuner, ed., *Christian Revelation and World Religions*, 1967, p. 52).

It is to be emphasised that this group of catholic theologians are not slipping into the kind of liberal view we have already considered and found unsatisfactory. They are united in two convictions. First, whoever is saved and whatever his religion, inside or outside the Church, salvation is always and only through Christ. He is the one, the only, Saviour and Mediator. And second, this more positive attitude to other faiths, distinct both from the early rigid and the later liberal view, does not make missions superfluous. Rather the contrary. The Christian tells others of Christ not primarily in order that they may be saved—this is God's affair—but because Christ's love constrains him to do so, because it would be unforgivable to keep silence about the wonderful things God has done in the life and death and resurrection of Jesus, because he is God's gift beyond words, because the Gospel has to be proclaimed. The salvation of men and races lies in the hands of God, not of his Church. But in this world and throughout history the Church's task is to make known all that has happened in Christ and all that is available in Christ. The motivation is not ultimate salvation but immediate and compulsive love. The Church therefore must evangelise and bear witness to Christ. The Church's life is that of a minority on behalf of the majority. This positive way of thinking about other religions does not mean the abandonment of the Church's missionary motive but its restatement. The Church has to be concerned with men as they are now, with the meeting of their needs, the establishment of peace and justice at all levels, the provision of a faith to live by, the making real of a present salvation which is a radical healing of individuals and communities. The destiny of men and nations is determined by God and is in his hands alone. The Church's mission is made necessary by the present not the future. The Christian dares to approach men of other faiths not because of the imperfection of their belief or practice but because of the sheer wonder of Jesus Christ.

We are leaving our discussion of evangelism and dialogue to the next lecture but certain practical points may be noted here in conclusion. First, it may be wise today to avoid all negative attitudes and negative statements. This may mean dropping such phrases as 'non-Christian religions' and even 'non-Christians'. We would do this not in order to blurr very real distinctions, which would be absurd, but to refrain from giving offence and making the wrong kind of judgments on others. I was once in an audience which was somewhat startled to hear Professor Ninian Smart refer to Christianity as the greatest of the non-Buddhist religions.

Second, we should seek to realise that although Christ is not *known* everywhere he *is* everywhere. As Christians we are called to make him known, not to make him present. The presence of Christians in a place can interpret and make explicit the presence of Christ. Our role is like that of John the Baptist whose message was: 'Among you stands one whom you do not know ... Behold, the Lamb of God, who takes away the sin of the world' (John 1. 26, 29). Similarly at Athens the apostle Paul said: 'What therefore you worship as unknown, this I proclaim to you' (Acts 17. 23). 'The Christian attitude is not ultimately one of bringing Christ *in*—but of bringing him *forth*' (Raymond Panikkar, *The Unknown Christ of Hinduism*, 1964, p. 45).

Third, for Christians to be content with leaving all other men to the religions they inherit would be to set up another form of apartheid, religious not racial. It would be to deny the universality of the Church, of the new Being, in which 'there is no such thing as Jew and Greek, slave and free-man, male and female; for you are all one person in Christ Jesus' (Gal. 3. 28). As Kenneth Cragg has said so finely: 'Baptism, bringing persons within the Church, means their incorporation by faith into the supranational fellowship of Christ. It does not, properly understood, de-culturalise the new believer; it enchurches him ... Conversion is not "migration": it is the personal discovery of the meaning of the universal Christ within the old framework of race, language, and tradition' (K. H. Cragg, *The Call of the Minaret*, 1956, p. 336). In other words, we cannot have historic Christianity, as the Church has understood it, without an overwhelming missionary obligation, because if Christ is

what the apostles claimed him to be, of universal significance, he is for everyman everywhere. To believe this and
to communicate it is what differentiates the Gospel from
other faiths.

V. CHALLENGES TO THE CHRISTIAN MISSION

THERE have always been challenges to the Christian Gospel from the first day it was preached until now. It goes without saying that those who reject the Gospel resent its missionaries. Within the Church there has always been a substantial number of people indifferent to its mission while accepting its general teaching. The rise of the modern missionary movement at the end of the eighteenth century led to some bitter criticism and cynicism. In a study of the public image of the missionary, Max Warren gives some spicy quotations from Sydney Smith, writing in 1808, later to be a Canon of St. Paul's, who contributed regularly to the *Edinburgh Review*. He concludes that this clergyman, who had the pen of a ready writer and wit, helped to form the images of the missionary 'as being somewhat paradoxically, a stupid and presumptuous person and at the same time a threat to the security of empire' (Max Warren, *Social History and Christian Mission*, 1967, p. 63). But such attacks on mission were mostly from either outside or the periphery of the Church. Today, however, the very concept of mission is being challenged or radically changed from within the Church. We have already noticed that some reputable theologians, otherwise orthodox in their beliefs, are querying any evangelistic approach to men of other faiths. We must now turn our attention to the various attacks on the whole idea of mission as evangelism. The mood of the Church seems to have changed; to use a musical analogy we have passed from a major into a minor key; the confidence of a century ago has been replaced by uncertainty and hesitation today.

One way of charting this change of mood is to listen to the successive pronouncements on mission during the last sixty years. In 1910 there was the great missionary conference at Edinburgh which is usually seen as the beginning of the ecumenical movement. It is almost impossible to recapture the exhilaration of that conference, the first of its kind on such a scale. The opening sentence of the popular report reads: 'The part that the world-wide enterprise of Christian missions is playing in moulding the history of the world is already a large one, and is destined to increase more and more' (W. H. T. Gairdner, *Edinburgh 1910*, p. 9). This was not an exaggeration then, but no-one would or could write like that now. The conference was hopeful and registered its conviction that 'the Church is confronted today, as in no previous generation, with a literally world-wide opportunity to make Christ known'. One speaker envisaged a Christendom of the Far East added to the Christendom of the West, held apart only by the wedge of Islam. A trebling of the missionary force was proposed. The possibility of evangelising the world in a generation was taken seriously. 'The concern of Christians should not be, lest non-Christian peoples refuse to receive Christ, but lest they, in failing to communicate him, will themselves lose him.'

The next international missionary conference was at Jerusalem in 1928. The situation had changed, for the First World War had broken the optimism which Edinburgh 1910 inherited from the nineteenth century and brought much disillusionment. There had also been the rise of theological liberalism, which in turn affected the missionary movement and its aims. At Jerusalem the missionary message could no longer be taken for granted. New attitudes to the other religions were in evidence, and the uniqueness of the Gospel was being questioned. It is salutary to remember that as long ago as 1928 Christian leaders were well aware of secular man and the challenge of secularism. The conference itself did not accept the current liberalism, believing that the revelation of Christ was still the basis of Christian mission. 'Coming into fellowship with Christ we find in ourselves an overmastering impulse to share him with others. We are constrained by the love of Christ and by obedience to his last command . . .'

The third conference in the series was at Tambaram, Madras, in 1938. By this time Karl Barth's influence was being felt and there was reaction from some of the more extreme liberal views expressed at Jerusalem. Hitler was in power in Germany, and many could see war clouds on the horizon. The voice of Hendrik Kraemer was dominant; there was a return to Biblical realism—Kraemer's phrase— and something of the sense of urgency felt at Edinburgh. These three World Missionary Conferences form a class on their own; there has been nothing of this kind since.

They were followed by a further series of three on a considerably smaller scale. In 1947 the Committee of the International Missionary Council met at Whitby, Ontario. Their theme was 'Christian Witness in a Revolutionary World'. It was the first world gathering of Christians after the end of the Second World War. The phrase 'expectant evangelism' was used. They stressed their conviction that the whole Church must be recalled to its primary missionary task, evangelism. There were echoes of the old slogan 'the evangelisation of the world in this generation', and the conference went on record as believing it possible 'that before the present generation has passed away, the Gospel should be preached to almost all the inhabitants of the world in such a way as to make clear to them the issue of faith or disbelief in Jesus Christ.' There was an emphasis on the responsibility of laymen in evangelism and on the partnership of Churches.

Before the next conference at Willingen in 1952, three international events had helped to change the missionary perspectives. There was the Palestine war in 1948–9, resulting in the creation of the state of Israel and the anger of the whole Arab world. There was the communist liberation of China in 1949–50 and the subsequent exclusion of all foreign missionaries. And there was the outbreak of the Korean war which continued from 1950–4. Willingen therefore approached its theme 'The Missionary Obligation of the Church' in a more sombre and less exultant spirit than at Whitby. In a notable address Max Warren pointed out how at Whitby it was felt that the most testing days were behind, at least for a generation, but at Willingen there was a realisation that the most testing days were immediately ahead. He was right. One of the speeches was given by Baron Reinold von Thadden, the founder of the Kirchentag movement in Germany. His subject was 'The Church under the Cross', which gave its title to the full report.

Undoubtedly his word made a great impact and led to the rapid development of the concept of the servant Church. The Cross determines the form of the Church, and 'a Church under the Cross cannot present itself other than in the form of a servant'. At the same time Willingen re-affirmed the Gospel and their commitment to preach it to every creature, noting the urgent need in the new situation for 'unofficial' missionaries.

The third and last conference of the International Missionary Council was in Ghana at the turn of the year 1957–8. Here the main issue was to decide on its integration with the World Council of Churches. The relationship since the W.C.C. was formed had been one of association. The other discussions reflected the beginning of a new self-questioning in the missionary movement. We are still in this phase. The proposed integration of the I.M.C. and the W.C.C. went through at New Delhi in 1961 and the idea was generally accepted that because mission and unity are related concerns, they must necessarily be the responsibility of one organisation. This, of course, is open to question and some of the early enthusiasts are beginning to have second thoughts.

Within the structure of the World Council of Churches the work of the I.M.C. was assigned to the Commission on World Mission and Evangelism, whose first meeting was held in Mexico City in 1963. This conference popularised the slogan 'Witness in Six Continents', a theologically impeccable assertion, but one which has led to confusion when applied to mission by failing to allow for the enormous differences between the six continents in terms of Christian resources already available in each. No responsible church leader today would deny that Europe and North America are as much areas of mission as are Asia and Africa, and in this respect our understanding of mission has changed considerably from that of a century ago. But is there no difference between those areas in which Christ has been preached and known for centuries and those in which he has never been preached? Is there no difference between countries where there is a substantial minority of practising Christians and at least one church in every town and village, and countries where only a tiny fraction of the community are

Christians and there is no organised church covering the whole territory? Is there no difference between a society in which the name and the claims of Jesus Christ are familiar even if rejected, and a society in which there is no means of learning about him because the Church is not yet visibly there? Neat slogans must not obscure hard facts.

This confusion was much in evidence at the Fourth Assembly of the World Council of Churches held in Uppsala in July 1968. When the draft section on Mission was published early in 1968 Donald McGavran, the American missionary writer, had reacted on behalf of the conservative evangelicals in a forthright article entitled: 'Will Uppsala Betray the Two Billion?' (Donald McGavran, *Church Growth Bulletin*, May 1968, Fuller Theological Seminary, California, U.S.A.). The concern behind this article was the enormous task of primary evangelism still confronting the Church. Population explosion had doubled the number since Edinburgh 1910, but the draft section had made no reference to this evangelistic task. When the subject was raised at Uppsala it led to heated debate and much misunderstanding on both sides. Those who took their stand with McGavran—and many of them were in no sense of the word conservative evangelicals—were accused of being traditionalists or lacking in social concern. Others were reluctant to make any distinction between the two billion without knowledge of Christ and the millions whose allegiance to him is nominal and whose lives deny him. There were many, including representatives from 'the third world', who did not wish their situation to be isolated in this manner and insisted that mission should be directed to the world of three billion, not two, in other words the whole world. One of the best statements of this position has been made by Dr. Eugene Smith who points out the dangers of white superiority being assumed in an evangelistic call which focuses on the two billion but forgets the lapsed millions of Christendom. 'A considerable proportion of the white population is composed of nominal Christians. Most of the coloured people are not Christian. Is there no need for true evangelism among the white "Christians" of South Africa who support apartheid; among the white "Christians" in Latin America who maintain corrupt, feudal oligarchies; among the "Christians" who support the neo-Nazi movement in Germany?' (E. L. Smith, *Church Growth Bulletin*, November 1968, p. 34). That this is true few would dispute. Nevertheless, it has to be pointed out that in this case Uppsala was curiously inconsistent, for again and again when viewed under other categories the third world *was* isolated. It was clearly identified as the area of poverty, hunger, and racial injustice. Speech after speech rightly reminded the Assembly of these things with a conviction which moved us in a way that none will soon forget. No-one had the effrontery to protest that there were 30 million destitute Americans in the richest country of the world, and that there were tens of thousands of poor and depressed people in Ireland, Sicily, and most countries of southern Europe, and that this should temper our total concern with the needs of the third world. The assumption was that, given the will, these countries had the resources for dealing with such problems in their own spheres. But no similar assumption was made in the case of the Church and its mission. This led to an apparent indifference, amounting to a loss of all sense of urgency, with regard to evangelism in places where the Church is small or does not exist at all. The result is that, whereas in some sections Uppsala said important and notable things, the section on mission was so eager to break with anything traditional that much of its report is thoroughly disappointing. There was compassion for the hungry—who would wish otherwise? There was no similar compassion for those without Christ, and although this was expressed by many delegates it did not find its way into the report. Judged by Uppsala the Roman Catholic Church at Vatican II and the conservative evangelicals outside the W.C.C. will take the main responsibility for world evangelism in the next few years. Commenting on Uppsala's attitude to mission, Sir Kenneth Grubb, a prominent layman with a record of work for international peace and justice, has said that if this approach were to gain further ground, 'it would cut the nerve of missionary obedience. The very nature of the Gospel is at stake. Today the very existence of Good News for all is called in question. If we cannot say with total conviction that Jesus of Nazareth is for all men and every man then we have little left worth

saying. The service we can offer to alleviate the most des-
perate needs of human-kind is no substitute for this Good
News. Neither can the preaching of the Gospel be a substitute for giving bread to the hungry. We are called to be
concerned with both—as our Master was' (Presidential
Address to the Annual Meeting of the Church Missionary
Society, 6 May 1969). It will be clear that Uppsala 1968
marks a very different attitude to evangelism from that of
Edinburgh 1910 and all the intervening conferences. Some
would say it reached an all-time low, indicating the missionary bankruptcy of the more extreme forms of radical
theology. But the purpose of this discussion of thinking
about mission from Edinburgh to Uppsala is to show that,
in a quite new way, a substantial challenge to mission
comes from inside the Church.

We must now turn to other aspects of this challenge.
First, there is the situation that has been reaching an
organised climax in the last few decades, when missions
have given way to churches and the emphasis has shifted
from foreign to indigenous. All this was wholly desirable
and has long been a primary aim of missionary policy. But
the result has been rather unexpected. When that far-
seeing missionary statesmen, Henry Venn, coined his
famous phrase 'the euthanasia of the mission', he did not
mean the end of mission as such but the end of mission as a
foreign structure scaffolding the Church. Too often, however, the end of missionary leadership has meant the end of
missionary activity altogether in the evangelistic sense. Professor H-W. Gensichen of Heidelberg has remarked: 'The
fact remains that even today the mission agencies are relatively unable to transmit the missionary impulse either to
the Churches in the West or to the younger Churches with
the result that the great missionary awakening for which
everyone longs has not come. Foreign missions continue to
produce younger Churches but very little "younger mission", and all too often, both at home and abroad, the
mission even seems to be dying in the arms of the Church'
(Hans-Werner Gensichen, *Living Mission*, Philadelphia,
1966, p. 15). This observation would not be equally true
everywhere, but it applies to enough churches to arouse
concern. It is easy to supply reasons and excuses. The so-

CHALLENGES TO THE CHRISTIAN MISSION

called younger Churches have had their hands full of problems. They have inherited a western-type organisation which they have to work. They have had to adjust to a post-colonial situation and find a new relationship between church and newly independent state. They have had to produce their own representatives for the ever-increasing number of international and ecumenical meetings and often these are those who can least be spared from responsible positions in their own countries. They have had to cope with poverty, civil wars, military coups, social change, and the familiar brands of revolution. They have had to keep the ship afloat. Eloquent lip-service has been paid to the primacy of evangelism but there has been far less life-service. Yet,

> 'The Church must be forever building, for it is forever
>   decaying within and attacked from without.
> For this is the law of life; and you must remember that
>   while there is time of prosperity
> The people will neglect the Temple, and in time of
>   adversity they will decry it.'

These lines of T. S. Eliot may be variously interpreted, but if his analysis is correct it follows that mission is the only form in which the Church can survive and grow. Without it the Church rapidly becomes stagnant.

It is fashionable these days, especially with ecclesiastical tourists, to denounce the Churches of the West and to set all their hope on the younger Churches whose services, in many countries, are so much better attended. But this is to be as shallow as the vicar who sees signs of revival if occasionally his church, seating three hundred people, is full but who forgets the other twenty thousand parishioners. Just as there is a vast amount of nominal Christianity in the West, so there is in the younger Churches. Uppsala was entirely right to insist that evangelism has to be directed to church members as well as to those outside. But the problem of so many younger Churches is lack of resources for the missionary task in their own borders. The mere existence of a church, a diocese, a province, is no guarantee of mission or of outreach. The need today is for those Churches which have resources available—and these are not only the Churches of the West—to offer them freely for service within churches where there are severe shortages. This is the meaning of *mutual* responsibility. The problem for the Churches which make these offers is to learn how to stimulate mission but not to dominate it, how to be colleagues but not to be substitutes.

Mission is also challenged by a general revulsion to propaganda. Never before in the history of man has the individual been the object of so much pressure to buy things, to belong to things, to believe this, to subscribe to that. Propaganda threatens not only our privacy but our very selfhood; it sometimes reaches a scale that can be an assault on human dignity. Until the age of mass communications the range and the agents of propaganda were strictly limited. This is no longer so. But mission is one particular kind of propaganda. It is one form of interference, and although it is not intended to deprive people of their liberty it certainly invades it. As an English word 'propaganda' derives from the *congregatio de propaganda fide* which the Roman Catholic Church set up in Rome in 1622. Gradually the term is acquiring a pejorative sense in modern use. How are we to respond to this new situation? It would be dishonest to pretend that mission, particularly evangelism, is not propaganda in *some* sense and that it has to compete with the propaganda of a good deal else. And yet, if the Christian Gospel cannot be seen to be different in kind from all other forms of propaganda, both by the way it is propagated and the results it achieves, we cannot expect much of a future for Christianity.

Propaganda involves an interplay of words and persons, and where it does without persons, as on posters and press advertisements, it seldom does without any words. In the case of religion both are essential. The danger with persons is that those who propagate will seem superior; the danger with words is that they will ring hollow. All engaged in evangelism need to be warned of these two factors. It may be helpful to recall how we ourselves react when accosted by a member of some sect or party of which we disapprove. Most of us have been exposed to visits by Jehovah's Witnesses or Mormons. We may admire their zeal but we do not like their doctrines or their persistence. They imply that we are in the wrong, that we are missing something they have, that we cannot really know God or live the good life except by throwing in our lot with their organisation. This seems arrogant and ridiculous. But this is precisely the impression many ardent Christians leave behind when they give their witness to those of other faiths or of none. Unless we admit it and face the challenge of it there is little hope of progress. The singer can ruin the song.

But the song itself can mean one thing to the singer and something else to the audience. Words convey varieties of meaning determined not by the speaker but by the hearer. Words like 'father', 'love', 'work', 'pleasure', will evoke quite different responses depending on the background and experiences of those who hear them. Words are sacred, but too often they are used glibly. What Jesus said about praying may apply equally to preaching and witnessing: 'In your prayers do not go babbling on like the heathen, who imagine that the more they say the more likely they are to be heard' (Mt. 6. 7). In evangelism verbal restraint promises to be more effective than effusion. But because Christian leaders speak and preach so often and some eager Christians give their witness with such ease, the quality suffers and gives place to triviality. This is not the way of effective evangelism. If we are to be taken seriously we should have the strength of character to refuse to speak too much, and the clergy should resist invitations to 'say a few words' at this and that. The alternative is that among the intelligent our words will receive even less attention than the latest television commercials about detergents.

Evangelism then is propaganda and bears the hazard of all propaganda. But in so far as it is Christian it will be distinct from all other propaganda. Its aim is not to elicit a response to us but a response to God. Its subject matter is the new humanity that God has brought about in Jesus Christ. As the Uppsala report says: 'Our part in evangelism might be described as bringing about the occasions for men's response to Jesus Christ.' As with prayer so with evangelism, the intention will be ceaseless but not the words.

Closely related to the modern abhorrence of propaganda is the similar distaste for proselytism. What we call evan-

gelism and regard as a good thing, adherents of other religions—and sometimes of other churches—call proselytism
and regard as a bad thing. It is never easy to clarify the
difference between the two and Lesslie Newbigin has con-
fessed that at the end of many discussions 'one is inclined
to conclude that the only workable distinction is that evangelism is what we do and proselytism is what others do' (op.
cit., p. 88). Originally a proselyte simply meant a convert to
Judaism. In its Greek form it was the most frequent Sep-
tuagint translation for the Hebrew word *gēr*, which meant
a resident alien, one who had come into the community
from outside. Christian converts do not seem to have been
called proselytes. Today proselytism is used almost invariably
in a derogatory sense and no reputable Christian church
would wish to call itself a proselytising body. Proselytising
is set over against the great commission to evangelise. The
main distinction is that proselytism has a coercive element
about it and seeks to impose its views on others, to make
stereotypes. Evangelism insists on leaving the recipients free
to respond as they will; it is an exercise in hope. As J. C.
Hoekendijk has put it: 'To evangelise is to sow and wait in
respectful humility and in expectant hope: in humility, because the seed that we sow has to die; in hope, because we
expect that God will quicken this seed and give it its proper
body' (J. C. Hoekendijk, *The Church Inside Out*, London,
1967, p. 21).

There is a tendency in some writers to equate all evangelism which has conversion in view with proselytism. In
two successive books J. G. Davies has a chapter on defective
concepts of mission. One of these defective concepts is
church-extension, which we shall consider in the next
lecture; the other is proselytism. Much of Davies's argument is valuable and cogent. He says that 'to preach Christianity and to preach Christ are not identical—the one is a
system of thought and practice, the other is the revelation
of a person' (J. G. Davies, *Worship and Mission*, London,
1966, p. 56; cf. *Dialogue with the World*, London, 1967,
p. 47 and pp. 46–57 where large sections are identical). But in
order to follow Hoekendijk and claim that 'evangelism is
indeed the opposite of passing on propaganda' (*Worship
and Mission*, p. 57) Davies has to deprive evangelism of any

connexion with making converts. In his view to make converts, or to seek to do so, *is* to proselytise, and he would like the term conversion dropped from the Christian vocabulary (*Dialogue*, p. 54). Let us admit that the Christian missionary enterprise is not guiltless in respect of proselytism. Davies is right to draw attention to this. But misuse need not be met by disuse. And Davies constantly seems to confuse converts to Christian and western culture, which must never be the aim of evangelism, with converts to Jesus Christ which must be its only aim. These charges that the making of converts is a defective concept of mission are usually made by western Christians who have not been converted from one of the great religions to Christ. Those who have come out of Hinduism of Buddhism or Islam into Christian faith often have criticisms to make about the western inclination to put faith and culture in the same package, but they do not decry conversion. Like St. Paul many of them had to write off everything else for the sake of gaining Christ, and they knew what they were doing.

In the New Testament conversion clearly involved two things. It meant joining the Christian community, and it meant experiencing in some sense the saving power of God through Christ. Those who proclaimed the Gospel and engaged in evangelising were not in the first place seeking to add to the numbers of the Church or to save souls. As D. T. Niles once said, mission is not a population drive for heaven. The Gospel was proclaimed because those who had responded to it wanted to share with others the best they knew. If this is propaganda, so be it. Saving of one's soul and joining the Christian Church are not the object of evangelism or the *esse* of conversion; they are results. Neither of these things must be put at the centre. 'Conversion is a turning round in order to participate by faith in a new reality which is the true future of the whole creation ... Conversion means being so turned round that one's face is towards that "summing up of all things in Christ" which is promised, and of which the resurrection of Jesus is the sign and first-fruit. It means being caught up into the activity of God which is directed to that end' (Lesslie Newbigin, *International Review of Missions*, Vol. LIV, No. 214, 1965, p. 149). The danger is not in linking conversion with salvation but in linking it exclusively with the idea of 'being saved'. For to be converted means membership of the saved and saving community, being a sharer in God's total work of salvation in the whole life of man and the world, not by migrating from humanity in order to enter the Church but by migrating more fully into humanity through incorporation into the new humanity of Christ.

A variant on this theme of opposing evangelism and conversion was produced by a Danish missionary, Kaj Baago of Bangalore, in 1966 (see his article, 'The post-Colonial Crisis of Missions', *International Review of Missions*, LV, No. 219, 1966). He questioned whether Buddhists, Hindus, and Muslims need become Christians in order to belong to Christ. By this he meant joining church organisations, adopting Christian traditions and customs, often more rooted in western culture than in the Gospel. He urged that the missionary task was no longer to draw men out of their religions into Christianity, but to leave Christianity and enter Hinduism and Buddhism, accepting these religions as one's own in so far as they do not conflict with Christ, and seeing them as the framework of the Gospel in Asia in which Jesus can again become incarnate. There seems some confusion here between what the missionary should do and what the prospective convert should do. No clear distinction is made between conversion to Christ and conversion to a western form of Christianity. Much of Baago's argument rests on his assertion that 'Christ himself belonged to a non-Christian religion', he remained within Judaism and he did not attempt to convert non-Jews to Judaism. The value of Baago's contribution is that it forces attention to all the encumbrances which have got tangled up with the Christian mission during the colonial period. But the remedy he proposes can hardly be taken seriously by any who accept the biblical doctrine of the Church. Bishop Newbigin, working in the same South India situation, reaches a very different conclusion. 'It would be equally pertinent to put the question the other way round and ask: "Can a Hindu who has been born again in Christ by the work of the Holy Spirit be content to remain without any visible solidarity with his fellow-believers?" The answer to that question is No. The New Testament knows nothing of a relationship with Christ which is purely mental and spiritual, unembodied in any of the structures of human relationship' (*The Finality of Christ*, p. 106).

There are two further challenges to missionary evangelism which we must look at: they are the new emphases on dialogue and on service. When rightly and theologically understood both these are important aspects of mission. The danger arises when either receives an exclusive emphasis.

Dialogue is a highly fashionable word just now and is used by many on every possible occasion. It would be a pity if a word with such specific meaning was spoiled and devalued by being overworked. Basically it means conversation, discussion. This is what St. Paul engaged in in Athens, Corinth, and Ephesus (Acts 17. 17; 18. 4; 19. 8). The essence of dialogue is that it should be open-ended and non-judgmental with a desire for mutual understanding. When the dialogue is between two men or groups of different faiths it takes on a particular seriousness. There are certain rules or conditions of effective dialogue. 1. Each partner must believe that the other is speaking in good faith. 2. Each partner must have a clear understanding of his own faith. 3. Each partner must seek a clear understanding of the other's faith, which means being willing to interpret that faith at its best, not its worst, and being ready to revise one's understanding of it. 4. Each partner must accept responsibility for what his group has done and is doing to foster unnecessary divisions. 5. Each partner must face the issues which cause separation as well as those which create unity. 6. Each partner must recognise that all that can be done with the dialogue is to offer it up to God. (This summary of the statement by Robert McAfee Brown appears in Roland de Corneille: *Christians and Jews*, New York, 1966, p. 88 f.)

Sometimes dialogue has been regarded in a way which for the Christian would amount to compromise. It is one thing for a Christian to have a conversation with someone of another faith (or of no faith) and to be ready to learn from him, to be introduced to new experiences and understanding, to gain a new respect for that man's convictions, and even to reach a deeper knowledge of his own faith by such an encounter. It is a different thing for a Christian who has experienced the grace of Christ, the love of God, and the fellowship of the Holy Spirit, to enter into dialogue as if all this experience were of no account and must be left behind, as if his belief in the finality and all-sufficiency of Christ had to be renounced or set on one side. In true dialogue we do not divest ourselves of our faith; we try to divest ourselves of our prejudices, particularly about the other person. We do not use the dialogue as an occasion for propaganda or proselytism in the crude sense of these words, but as Christians we would be untrue to our Lord and irresponsible to the other man if within the dialogue we did not bear witness when the right occasion presented itself. The main feature of dialogue is that it is not monologue. It is in this respect that 'dialogue and proclamation are not the same. The one complements the other in a total witness' (Uppsala Report, p. 29). The Uppsala statement is of great value. 'A Christian's dialogue with another implies neither a denial of the uniqueness of Christ, nor any loss of his own commitment to Christ, but rather that a genuinely Christian approach to others must be human, personal, relevant, and humble. In dialogue we share our common humanity, its dignity and fallenness, and express our common concern for that humanity. It opens the possibility of sharing in new forms of community and common service. Each meets and challenges the other; witnessing from the depths of his existence to the ultimate concerns that come to expression in word and action.' Dialogue may not normally be the context for Christians to seek conversions, for this could be self-defeating. Dialogue is the way of removing misunderstanding, of establishing common trust and relationship. It is a recognition that evangelism can never be casual or haphazard or impersonal. Even proclamation can be made in the spirit of dialogue and can happen within it. There can be no conversion without conversation. Long before Christians can evangelise they must be able to converse. But conversation of this kind is not an end in itself: the end for both participants is a deeper discovery of God and his will and whatever that may lead to.

Service, like dialogue, is a profoundly necessary Christian activity and much less difficult. It is open to all and does not require special training and expertise. In an earlier lecture we have examined the biblical concept of *diakonia*. No-one today is likely to question that the Church must engage in many forms of service for the relief of human need and the betterment of mankind. Millions live in sub-human conditions. Helder Camara, the Roman Catholic Archbishop of Recife in north-east Brazil, constantly pleads for these in his human and revolutionary speeches, describing 'the man who depends entirely on the property owner, who lives on his land in a miserable hut, receives a wretched wage which permits him to stave off starvation and wears rags for clothes, who can be sacked without notice—such a man is incapable of man-to-man or brother-to-brother relationship with his employer. He is rather in the position of a slave to his master' (Helder Camara, *Church and Colonialism*, London, 1969, p. 74). Colin Morris, while President of the United Church of Zambia, wrote with a pen dipped in fire this opening paragraph to a disturbing book: 'The other day a Zambian dropped dead not a hundred yards from my door. The pathologist said he'd died of hunger. In his shrunken stomach were a few leaves and what appeared to be a ball of grass. And nothing else' (Colin Morris, *Include Me Out!*, London, 1968, p. 7). Barbara Ward at Uppsala made one of the most moving and brilliant speeches I have ever heard on world poverty. It would be so easy to respond, as many in fact propose, by urging the Church to put its *total* energies and resources into relief work and to interpret mission *exclusively* in terms of service. The supreme achievement of Uppsala was to focus the attention of the whole Church on to this problem, and unquestionably it is the duty of every church to do more than it has ever done before in meeting human need on this enormous scale. But does this exhaust the meaning of mission? J. G. Davies, for example, thinks that service *is* proclamation. 'To participate in that activity is to join in a non-verbal proclamation' (*Dialogue with the World*, p. 17). Now it is perfectly true that in Christ the Word is accompanied by action. This we have already seen repeatedly. What Davies does not sufficiently recognise is that in Christ the action is interpreted by the Word. Jesus fed the multitude. But in St. John's gospel he goes on to speak to them about living bread, about faith, about his own flesh given for the life of the world. Feeding hungry people is a Christian thing to do and we must do it.

But it is not gospel. It is one part of mission but it is not the whole. And is the Gospel only for the two out of three who are poor and not for the one in three who is rich? If, as we must hope and pray, world poverty has been largely abolished within a generation, does this mean that the Christian mission will have been completed? Did Jesus come only to supply man's material needs and give him a happier human existence? This is not the Gospel declared in the New Testament. The end of poverty will not mean the end of sin. And when all the problems which haunt us today— hunger, racism, war—are solved, man will still stand in need of forgiveness, of hope beyond the grave, and of entering the new humanity this side of it. The Gospel is concerned with these things above all else, but not apart from all else. Service alone is no substitute for evangelism.

We conclude by reaffirming that nothing that has happened to the Church or to the world in the twentieth century relieves it of the burden to evangelise. Mission and evangelism are not the same. Mission includes evangelism but also a great deal more. Whereas all evangelistic activity may rightly be described as missionary, not all missionary activity could properly be described as evangelistic. Evangelism is one activity of the Church but mission is meant to be its very condition. Could it not be said that the Church is *in mission* as a planet is *in orbit*? We are committed to evangelism because we are committed to one who says to individuals in every age, 'follow me'. And to those who follow he says 'I will make you fishers of men ... From henceforth you will catch men ... the gospel must first be preached to all nations ... make disciples of all nations' (Mk. 1. 17; Lk. 5. 10; Mt. 28. 19). Some of the latest ecumenical documents do not quote these words, but they remain written, and they are still being heard.

An impressive statement about evangelism is appended as a postscript to a notable series of recent Bampton Lectures. 'I must hope that the lectures do reflect and convey my conviction that the things concerning Jesus are of central and decisive importance in putting us on to the realities of man's situation with regard to the world and God. Since I suffer from the further conviction that reality must be faced, I naturally believe and desire that others should see and be convinced of those realities about God and man which are demonstrated in Jesus and pointed to by Jesus. This desire of mine is reinforced by the evident fact that what is declared about reality by and through Jesus is realistic and practical good news about the possibilities and direction of human fulfilment. The things concerning Jesus constitute and imply a universal Gospel the contents of which are so humanly worth while that it would demonstrate the extreme of inhumanity not to wish urgently to share this good news. Hence I find myself under precisely the same command and obligation to "preach the gospel" as did the Christians of New Testament times' (David Jenkins, *The Glory of Man*, London, 1967, p. 113).

VI. THE PROGRESS OF THE GOSPEL

ALL titles that include words like growth and progress are ambiguous and therefore suspect. Such concepts are relative and hard to assess accurately. God's thoughts and ways are not like ours and neither is his arithmetic. In the last century and well into this statistics of Church growth, the numbers of baptisms and ordinations, were confidently used as indicators of achievement or lack of it. While they still provide certain broad pointers which enable comparisons to be made between one situation or area and another, and for that reason they cannot be dismissed as valueless—they are the raw material for the sociologist of religion—nevertheless we recognise today that other factors have to be considered. Our concerns have to include renewal as well as extension, structures as well as persons. It is for this reason that we prefer to take as our final theme the progress of the Gospel rather than the growth of the Church or the spread of Christianity. The first alternative conjures up the idea of an institution acquiring more members and power, and the second tends to suggest the geographical spread of Christianity in a way that can be marked by a colour on a map. The basic question before us is how we are to analyse attainments of nineteen centuries and what we have a right to expect in the future. To use more theological language, what is the progress of the Gospel?

This phrase comes from St. Paul (Phil. 1. 12 R.V.) The Greek original, *prokopē*, occurs only twice elsewhere in the New Testament, each time in the Pauline corpus, and refers to the spiritual growth of the Philippian Church and of Timothy (Phil. 1. 25; 1 Tim. 4. 15). The word has a ring of pioneering, cutting forward a way of advance; it is progress by sustained effort rather than by inevitable evolution. In this sense there is a progress of the Gospel which is the proper concern of the Christian community. This is not to be identified with the growth of the institutional church or

the spread of Christianity across the world, but neither can
it be entirely divorced from these.

In the last lecture we noticed the marked change of mood
as between Edinburgh 1910 and Uppsala 1968. Edinburgh
inherited all the optimism of the Victorian era; nothing was
impossible. The missionary movement reflected this in its
unashamedly self-conscious triumphalism. Missionaries
were as convinced that their cause would be victorious as
communists are today. They saw the whole world being
won for Jesus Christ and they did not hesitate to use this
kind of language. The majority of Anglicans and mainline
protestants do not think like this any more, and no such
talk was heard at Uppsala. Although many a congregation
still sings heartily

> Boundless as ocean's tide
> Rolling in fullest pride,
> Through the earth far and wide
> Let there be light!

these sentiments and this language are somewhat strained
and inappropriate today. Does this therefore mean that the
Christian hope has changed its character? May we still
hope? Are the horizons of hope entirely other-worldly, beyond the grave and beyond history? Or can we believe that
the Christian mission will achieve real and lasting effects in
human life and in this world and in time? Are we right to
drop all the glad anticipations of our nineteenth-century
fathers and adapt to the more sombre climate of the last
third of the twentieth century? Are there any norms in the
Bible which can be guidelines of permanent validity?

In all this we are up against the problem of the pen-
dulum, the swing from one emphasis to its opposite, the
choice between the either and the or. Instead of that
enrichment which would come from incorporating new
ideas and recognitions into what is best in the old tradition
and accepting the consequences and the changes, too often
a total displacement of the old is preferred and there is an
exclusive concentration on the new. Thus today there is a
tendency in the new radicalism to insist that evangelism
must give way completely to service, proclamation to dia-

logue, mission aimed at persons to mission aimed at structures. A penitence for ineffectiveness becomes a rationalisa-
tion of failure, a belief in the power of the Gospel is replaced by a belief in the power of reformed organisations,
progress is decried and protest applauded, and the renewal
of humanity is considered independently from the revival
of the Church. It is now possible to attend Christian conferences where prayer is regarded as a waste of time, action
alone counts, and even then it is frequently just talk about
action. At the end of this route we may have to confess
with the poet Byron, 'I am ashes where once I was fire'. My
anxiety is not about a radicalism which returns to the roots
but about a radicalism which would destroy the roots.
Whereas in the furnishings of a room the antique and the
novel do not easily blend, in Christ we are confronted with
one who continually brings out of his treasure what is new
and what is old (Mt. 13. 52). The progress of the Gospel
requires both. In the Kingdom of God tradition and revolution are not mutually exclusive: both have their place.
The *Magnificat* certainly prescribes a very revolutionary
social programme, as many commentators have pointed
out, but it does this in the framework of a theological tradition with a long history. The greatness and the mercy of
God, the joy of his salvation and the holiness of his name,
all deeply traditional themes, are the context in which his
revolutionary deeds are sung (Lk. 1. 46-55). If the theological foundations had been overthrown the social
programme would have had no base. Theological anarchy
is not a soil which produces a missionary impulse.

In this lecture we must look at various aspects of the
relation between mission and history. Mission is not only
Christianity looking outward into the world but also looking forward into the future. It sees a future filled with
Christ and dominated by Christ. He is already Lord. He is
the Omega point to which all converge. His destiny is to
complete, to unify, to fill all things. Mission recognises this,
and by its missionary obedience the Church moves towards
it. In this sense Moltmann is not exaggerating when he
claims, 'the missionary direction is the only constant in history' (Jürgen Moltmann, *Theology of Hope*, London, 1967,
p. 284). The concept of mission in Christianity fills approxi-

mately the same role as the concept of revolution in Marxism and there are some fascinating parallels. Both take history seriously, both believe in the transformation of history, both see the need to work towards this and call for commitment to the cause, both look forward to a future in which peace and justice abound. The means by which the goal is reached are very different; so is the content of the end.

Using descriptive language of quite another kind Teilhard de Chardin shares the same vision. The end is the divine *milieu*, when God is all in all. This does not arrive without cost and effort, for 'our faith in the Kingdom of God has been disconcerted by the resistance of the world to good ... But in fact how many of us are genuinely moved in the depths of our hearts by the wild hope that *our* earth will be recast? Who is there who sets a course in the midst of our darkness towards the first glimmer of a *real* dawn? ... We persist in saying that we keep vigil in expectation of the Master. But in reality we should have to admit, if we were sincere, *that we no longer expect anything*. The flame must be revived at all costs. At all costs we must renew in ourselves the desire and hope for the great Coming. But where are we to look for the source of this rejuvenation? We shall clearly find it, first and foremost, in an increase of the attraction exercised directly by Christ upon his members. And then *in an increase of the interest*, discovered by our thought, in the preparation and consummation of the Parousia. And from where is this interest to spring? From the perception of *a more intimate connection* between the victory of Christ and the outcome of the work which our human effort here below is seeking to construct' (Pierre Teilhard de Chardin, *Le Milieu Divin*, London, 1960, p. 149 f.). In an earlier passage he writes: 'Under the influence of our faith, the universe is capable, without outwardly changing its characteristics, of becoming more supple, more fully animate—of being "sur-animated". That is the "at the most" and the "at the least" of the belief expressly imposed upon us by the Gospel' (ibid., p. 127). Again, 'Expectation—anxious, collective and operative expectation of an end to the world, that is to say of an issue for the world—that is perhaps the supreme Christian func-

tion and the most distinctive characteristic of our religion
... Christmas, which might have been thought to turn our
gaze towards the past, has only fixed it further in the
future. The Messiah, who appeared for a moment in our
midst, only allowed himself to be seen and touched for a
moment before vanishing once again, more luminous and
ineffable than ever, into the depths of the future. He came.
Yet now we must expect him—no longer a small chosen
group among us, but all men—once again and more than
ever. The Lord Jesus will only come soon if we ardently
expect him. It is an accumulation of desires that should
cause the Pleroma to burst upon us ... Only twenty centuries have passed since the Ascension. What have we made
of our expectancy?' (ibid., p. 148 f.). I quote Teilhard at this
length, not merely because of the hopefulness of his vision
and the beauty in which it is expressed, but because writing
primarily as a scientist and a mystic he is in fact emphasising the intimate relation of missionary obedience to the end
of history and the ultimate achievement of God's purpose
for mankind and the universe. The same point could have
been made by quoting one of the most baffling texts in the
New Testament 'And this gospel of the Kingdom will be
proclaimed throughout the earth as a testimony to all
nations; and then the end will come' (Mt. 24. 14; cf. Mk.
13. 10). Perhaps Teilhard's words cast some light on the
meaning of that text and make it a little less baffling. If we
are concerned about what happens in history, about the
fate of the next generation or of our own, we cannot as
Christians be indifferent to the progress of the Gospel.

   This brings us to another problem about history. Christians believe that Jesus is Lord and therefore Lord of
history. Israel had learned that Yahweh, unlike the *baalim*,
was not a local or a tribal or a nature God, but the Creator
of all things and the Lord over all events. Nothing happened without him. Jesus had said: 'Are not sparrows two a
penny? Yet without your Father's leave not one of them
can fall to the ground' (Mt. 10. 29). This is an assertion of
God's sovereignty and providence in contrast to determinism
or blind fate. But Christian theology has always drawn
a distinction between what God permits and what God
actively causes or prompts. We cannot say that God *caused*

six million Jews to perish under Hitler, and there are many other things that we can hardly attribute to the will of God as it has been revealed in Jesus Christ. The problem then is how to discern what is of God and what is not of God in the events of our time. Isaiah believed that God raised up the pagan empire of Assyria to be the rod of his anger and the staff of his fury against Israel (Isa. 10. 5). It would not have been easy for the average Jew to think like this, and as things turned out God did deliver Jerusalem from the hosts of Sennacherib. From one point of view Assyria represented judgment, from another salvation.

In our time there are movements and revolutions which appear not only to threaten the Church but to be working directly against all that the Gospel is meant to achieve for the benefit of mankind. Would we be justified in saying of Stalin's Russia, with all its brutality, what Isaiah said of Assyria? Is the resurgence of the great religions of Asia and their bitter resistance to the Gospel prompted by God? Bishop Newbigin has expressed the modern dilemma: 'If history is not a meaningless jumble of events, if God is working out a purpose in it, it is necessary to try to interpret —even if only in very modest, tentative, and provisional terms—what he is doing. If we are to know where to act, where to throw our weight, where to commit ourselves, we must have some provisional answer to the question: Where is God at work and where is the Devil?' (op. cit., p. 82). It is a relief to find someone honestly raising this point, because one of the most dangerous heresies of our day is the tacit assumption in some circles that God is equally at work in every revolution and in all the secularisation that is taking place.

The document issued by the World Council of Churches under the title *The Church for Others* (Geneva, 1967), important and challenging as it is, is not sufficiently clear at this point and may be responsible for some of our present confusion. It begins, rightly in my view, by recognising that secularisation is a fruit of the Gospel and by understanding secularisation as 'a liberation from the control of metaphysics and theology'. Water is H_2O not a chaos-goddess, and so on. We have to let the world be the world, the secular be the secular, and see Christ at work there. We need not ques-

tion the validity and the independence of the secular as
expounded by writers such as Harvey Cox and van
Leeuwen. Charles Davis, who does not lose sight of the
wood for the trees, has written : 'The secular is the domain
open to human investigation, the field where the enquirer
can expect the insight that masters its object and penetrates
its intrinsic truth' (Charles Davis, *God's Grace in History*,
London, 1966, p. 37). In contrast to this the sacred is the
area of mystery. But Davis argues that the recognition of
the autonomy of the secular in its own sphere does not
mean the elimination of the sacred (ibid., p. 52). It is precisely this tendency which one finds too often in writings
where the benefits of secularisation are stressed in a way
which would almost equate it with Christian salvation. This
is not wholly avoided in *The Church for Others* where all
that God is doing in history is seen as the *missio Dei*. The
group is right to distinguish the mission of God from the
missions of churches. To define the purpose of the *missio
Dei* they employ the Old Testament term *shalom* which
means far more than peace, for it includes righteousness,
truth, fellowship, all aspects of life in its fulness. Mission
therefore is seen as the Church's pointing to the signs of
God's *shalom* being established, as for example in 'the
emancipation of coloured races, the concern for humani-
sation of industrial relations, various attempts at rural development, the quest for business and professional ethics,
the concern for intellectual honesty and integrity' (op. cit.,
p. 15). The Church, we are reminded, is a segment of the
world which confesses the Lordship of Christ; it is *pars
pro toto*; it must live ex-centredly (p. 17 f.). True. But is it an
adequate definition of mission to say of the Church that 'it
has to seek out those situations in the world that call for
loving responsibility and there it must announce and point
to *shalom*' (p. 18). I confess that I find a sentence like this
singularly meaningless. What situations in the world do
not call for loving responsibility? Is loving responsibility
alone an accurate description of what the apostles thought
of the mission they had received from the risen Christ? Is
the Gospel (and the salvation it brings) no longer to be
concerned with the forgiveness of sin, the sanctification of
home and family, the promise of eternal life, none of which

can be regarded as the results of secularisation? At one time
it was necessary to remind people that the Gospel had social
implications; now the urgency is to recall them to its personal and moral elements. In a world where Christians are
divided over so many issues, even over questions of peace
and justice, and where there is no overwhelming consensus
of Christian opinion on such troubled situations as Viet-
nam, the Arab–Israeli conflict, the Nigerian civil war,
how does the Church or any particular group of Christians
attain a position of reasonable certainty about which side
represents God's will? Just to state the question shows its
naïveté. It also exposes the unsatisfactory nature of re-
interpreting mission as finding the places where God is at
work and joining in. What does this mean in concrete terms
and political realities? Does it mean doing what Ché
Guevara sought to do in the jungles of Bolivia or does it
mean trying to prevent another Cuba in Latin America?
Does it mean following a Martin Luther King in non-
violent protest of joining the militants who will go to all
lengths in the name of black power?

This whole approach is fallacious. Certainly the one and
only essential mission is God's and his servants are invited
to participate in it. Mission, God's redemptive action, describes one aspect of God's relation to his world, but he is
related to the world also as creator and sustainer and judge.
Not all events are mission. What is to be said of Belsen or
Hiroshima? We must avoid what has been called 'historical
pantheism', a failure to preserve the qualitative difference
between the action of God and the action of man. (Hel-
mut Flender, *St. Luke, Theologian of Redemptive History*,
London, 1967, p. 5.) History means secular history and in
this God is active. He is Lord. But he is not the sole agent at
work. History is ambivalent. 'The kingdom of heaven may
be compared to a man who sowed good seed in his field; but
while men were sleeping, his enemy came and sowed weeds
among the wheat, and went away ...' (Mt. 13. 24 f.). The
concept of 'the enemy' at work in history is not prominent
in contemporary theological writing, but it is remarkably to
the fore in fiction, poetry, and drama, all of which are grap-
pling with the problem of evil and of sin more honestly and
more passionately than some of our theologians. The events

described at the heart of the New Testament are secular events and part of secular history. Jesus was crucified under Pontius Pilate. The crucifixion shares the ambivalence of all secular events. Who was responsible? The Jewish leaders? Yes. They handed Jesus over to Pilate (Mk. 15. 1). The mob? Yes. They demanded that he should be crucified (Mk. 15. 13). The devil? Yes. Satan entered into the heart of Judas (Lk. 22. 3; Jn. 13. 27). God? Yes, Jesus reminded Pilate that he would have no power over him unless it had been given from above (Jn. 19. 11), and Paul asserted of the Crucifixion that God was in Christ reconciling the world to himself (2 Cor. 5. 19), and Peter spoke of Christ being given up to men by the deliberate will and plan of God (Acts 2. 23). We cannot therefore divide events into sacred and secular or see a stream of sacred history in the midst of secular history or give some special significance to the history of the Church as an institution. We can believe that God is active in history both through his people and outside his people. Sometimes we can see the marks of his activity in the triumph of goodness; sometimes like Gamaliel viewing the Christian movement in its earliest years we have to admit that we cannot tell if something is of God—we must wait and see. We certainly cannot take it upon ourselves to call everything of which we approve *missio Dei*. To do this is to use the word mission in a sense quite alien to its biblical traditional meaning. Better to have some reserve in saying what God's mission is than to be too dogmatic about it; we would be on safer ground to confess with Job 'Lo, these are but the outskirts of his ways; and how small a whisper do we hear of him! But the thunder of his power who can understand?' (Job. 26. 14). For us the main responsibility lies in discovering the meaning of our own participation in the mission of God.

The Dutch theologian, Hendrikus Berkhof, has a chapter with the fascinating title: The Missionary Endeavour as a History-Making Force (H. Berkhof, *Christ the Meaning of History*, London, 1966. With the coming of Christ, he writes, 'a new idea of *being human* is ushered in . . . The individual is recognised in his own significance. The human *personality* is respected. Particular attention is given to the suffering and the oppressed. An ordinary street scene, such as an ambulance stopping all traffic because *one* wounded man must be transported, is the result of the coming of the Kingdom' (p. 88). Berkhof adds: 'In order fully to understand the unprecedented revolution that being human experienced through the proclamation of Christ, one must have lived in a communistic world, in the lands of Islam, in Hinduism, or among primitive people' (p. 90 f.). Having travelled fairly extensively in three of these worlds I can endorse that. It is indeed by such experience of travel that the progress of the Gospel can to some extent be discerned, if not measured, and to have lived in a place where all through the centuries the name of Christ has never been heard is to temper all criticism of the Church and missions and institutional Christianity. The Gospel, after all, is not an idea but an event, the response to which means a new creation in the midst of the old. The Gospel cannot circulate the world disembodied. Neither can communism or democracy. If beliefs are to spread they have to be embodied and expressed in people who hold them. In the case of the Gospel this means the Church. For this reason the progress of the Gospel cannot be dissociated from the fortunes of the Church.

This brings us to an issue of current controversy. It is fashionable to be cynical about the Church, to distrust any power it may have, to be indifferent to its growth. Any concern with church growth is vigorously scorned in certain places. In its section on mission the Uppsala report goes so far as to qualify evangelistic concern for the non-Christian world because 'that concern becomes suspect when the church is preoccupied with its own numerical and institutional strength' (*The Uppsala 1968 Report*, p. 32). J. G. Davies deprecates all concentration on church extension as much as he deprecates proselytism (J. G. Davies, *Worship and Mission*, pp. 46 ff. *Dialogue with the World*, pp. 40 ff.). The prophet behind this line of thought is J. C. Hoekendijk whose writings have been very influential particularly in the study on the missionary structure of the congregation. Hoekendijk is a strong critic of all 'church-centric missionary thinking'. He finds that this has been prominent not only in the Roman Catholic Church, as exemplified by Père Charles, but also among protestants since Jerusalem 1928.

His own view is that the church has no fixed place in the world, it cannot be established, it *happens* only when it proclaims the Kingdom, it is purely functional and as such is a function of the apostolate (J. C. Hoekendijk, *The Church Inside Out*, London, 1967, p. 40 f.). The main aspect of Hoekendijk's protest is justified but it has been over-stated and yet more so by some of his disciples. Those who respond to Jesus Christ enter an already existing com-munity with a history and with world-wide connexions. Their own witness may well be given as laymen in diaspora and not as conscious agents of the Church. But if their faith is to be sustained and they are to have any kind of Chris-tian fellowship they are bound to have contact with the historic Church in one or other of its aspects, and this means the Church as an institution.

Church extension or growth need not in the first place mean an increase of Anglicans or Lutherans or some other denomination, and Davies is therefore right when he re-marks: 'Can anyone seriously maintain that mission, i.e. the divine activity in the world, is primarily directed to securing the increase of Methodists, Congregationalists and others?' (*Dialogue*, p. 41). But it may well be asked if any reputable leaders of churches or missionary societies within the ecumenical movement would define mission in such a way. Yet many of them would be concerned about the growth or the total Christian community in a place, not because they think God works *only* through the Christian community, but because the witness of the Bible makes it clear that God calls people to the knowledge of himself and that he gives to his people certain tasks to do as his ser-vants. We cannot therefore be indifferent whether or not he has those whom he can call 'my people' to work for him. Jesus came into the world to 'bring us to God' (1 Pet. 3. 18) and all else in the Christian mission is a by-product of this. Men and women who are brought to God, which is the first (but not the sole) aim of the mission, will join the Christian community in corporate expressions of their faith and wor-ship.

In the first days there was a real interest in the growth of that community. In *Acts* there are regular little reports with approximate figures. On the day of Pentecost 'those who accepted (Peter's) word were baptised, and some three thousand were added to their number that day' (2. 41). Later we are told that 'day by day the Lord added to their number those whom he was saving' (2. 47). Later still 'numbers of men and women were added to their ranks as believers in the Lord' (5. 14). A new section begins: 'During this period, when disciples were growing in number' (6. 1), and the results of the mission of Barnabas at Antioch are mentioned in these terms: 'Large numbers were won over for the Lord' (11. 24). There are other such references throughout *Acts*. In view of this it can hardly be seriously maintained that the Church is not meant to grow. If it does not grow, we must seek the reason why. Many of the images of the Church in the New Testament suggest growth. Altogether J. G. Davies, however, lists seven objections to the idea of church extension. He is concerned lest the evangelising group becomes a substitute for the message it has to proclaim. This concern is legitimate. But he goes on to say: 'Instead of calling men to accept the good news of the Kingdom, they are summoned to emigrate from the social structures of the world and enter into an alien community with all its cultural baggage' (*Dialogue*, p. 42). This is to make an unreal distinction which exists nowhere in the New Testament. Of course people must be summoned to hear the good news of the Kingdom, but those who respond to it have invariably joined with others who have responded to it. Often this has been at some cost, particularly to a Hindu, a Buddhist, or a Muslim, but what alternative is there? Can a Christian life be sustained outside the Church, without sacraments, without fellowship? The New Testament nowhere envisages such a possibility. It is therefore unrealistic to speak of emigrating from the social structures of this world and entering into an alien community, for this is precisely the meaning of Christian baptism. This is the very thing that has been done by Christians down the ages, and whenever I have asked a convert from Islam, Buddhism, or Hinduism, if they regretted doing what they had done, they have always replied that there was no alternative. Like Luther they would have to confess, Here I stand, I can no other. From the first days until now the Church has been accused of being alien. This

is true (1 Pet. 2. 11; Heb. 11. 13). But is not this part of the
scandal of the Gospel? The cultural baggage is unfortunate
and unnecessary; every effort is being made to dissociate
Christianity from this baggage. 'The cultural forms of the
bringing of the faith have no enduring right to become the
permanent forms of its accepting' (Kenneth Cragg: *Christianity in World Perspective*, London, 1968, p. 203). But
even when we succeed in getting rid of the cultural baggage
the newly embraced faith is just as alien and unpopular.
The Church in the last analysis is a community of aliens
looking for a home and it is impossible to have Christianity
without the Church or to retain the Church without concern that it should grow. The Church is lightly criticised
but it cannot be lightly dismissed. Where would we be
without it? In times of general instability such as our own
there is much to be said for a body with a solid institutional
form. As Leslie Paul has pointed out, 'the strenuous effort
men make to embody a church in unchanging forms and
institutions (including buildings and furniture) has the
deepest possible religious significance. It is a mere super-
ficiality if not superfluity to say that a thing has to change,
because society is changing, when what it is seeking to re-
present is non-change, endurance, the eternal' (Leslie Paul,
The Death and Resurrection of the Church, London, 1968,
p. 81).

Closely related to this question is that of mission to
structures. Many are saying today that the primary mission
of the Church is to the power structures, not to individuals
with a view to conversion. Undoubtedly there are a
number of situations where the Church has failed to challenge the power structures with the Gospel. But having
admitted this two qualifications have to be made. First, it is
impossible to make any impact upon structures until some
impact has been made on the persons living within them or
responsible for them, whether they be structures of government or industry or education or sport or entertainment. In
every sense persons take precedence over structures even if
structures dehumanise persons. Second, there are many
areas of mission in which it would be utterly impossible for
the Church to address the structures of society with the
Gospel. I recently attended a conference in the United

States where most of the young men and women straight from college and shortly destined for overseas service were obsessed with mission to structures, having renounced all thought of personal evangelism with a view to conversion. But sooner or later they will find, not without pain and perhaps disillusionment, that you just cannot do this everywhere. There can only be a mission to power structures in situations where the Christian community is strong enough, both numerically and morally, to make itself felt. Any Christian who enters Russia or Saudi Arabia or Thailand with the intention of addressing or changing the power structures will soon find himself either expelled or imprisoned. This kind of talk is sheer idealism which takes no account of political realities. It is precisely at this point that the progress of the Gospel is contingent upon the size and power of the Christian community, which the Uppsala report scorned. Where there is a substantial Christian minority or an articulate Christian public opinion, it is at least *possible* to challenge the power structures of a country or society. Where the Church is small and few, if any, Christians are in positions of influence within these structures, nothing can be done beyond prayer and witness. It is one thing to urge that the Church should interpret its mission in terms of structures in countries in Western Europe and North America, in Australasia and even in Southern Africa, because in all these areas there is a general recognition of Christianity by the state and the national leadership. It is on this ground that racism can be challenged in these countries in the name of Christ and appeals made for a constructive response to world poverty. But no such situation exists in Communist, Muslim or Buddhist countries, and even in India and Japan, where the general influence of the Gospel has been far deeper than might be supposed from the small proportion of Christians, it would be premature to speak of a mission to structures.

For all these reasons the growth of the Church and the number of converts to Christ *does matter* if there is to be any progress of the Gospel. To suppose anything else is to live in a world of make-believe far removed from the real missionary frontiers. In some places today the Church is growing noticeably: in Tanzania, in Indonesia, in Korea, in

Taiwan, not to mention others. It is growing among the Pentecostals in Latin America and in the Independent (breakaway) Churches all over Africa. There are pockets of growth where there is renewal in the West and elsewhere. But in too many places the Church has ceased to grow, and in some it has definitely begun to decline. We should not fail to note that although the great majority of the world's Christians are white-skinned and live in the West, the main growing points are among coloured peoples outside the West, and the most serious areas of decay and decadence are among whites and inside the West. The challenge to the West is to adjust from a Christendom-situation to a *diaspora*-situation. The challenge to the younger Churches is to emerge through growth into a situation where the Church, by its mission, can make its impact upon structures and the whole of society just as it has already made its impact upon thousands of individuals, and to do this without imitating the pre-suppositions of Christendom and seeking power in order to have influence. In our day, everywhere, the Church has to learn to exert influence without acquiring political power, to proclaim the Lordship of Christ by being totally available as his servant to all humanity. But it will not even be there, let alone available in servant form, if it renounces all thought of making converts or of numerical and spiritual growth. Karl Rahner, one of the greatest contemporary Roman Catholic scholars, has written: 'Our *diaspora* situation is not just a fact but a "must" in the history of salvation ... We cannot cease to be missionary; we have to want the number of Christians to increase, to want their influence, their importance, the concrete realisation of a Christian spirit in public affairs and social institutions to grow; we have to try to diminish the contrary of these things. But despite all this, our growing *diaspora* situation is something to be expected, something foretold, something we can count on and which need not cause us any inner conflict or missionary defeatism' (Karl Rahner S. J., *Mission and Grace*, Vol. I, London, 1963, p. 39 f.). And he goes on to say: 'Let us get away from the tyranny of statistics. For the next hundred years they are always going to be against us, if we ever let them speak out of turn. *One* real conversion in a great city is something

more splendid than the spectacle of a whole remote village
going to the sacraments. The one is an essentially religious
event, a thing of grace; the other is to a large extent a
sociological phenomenon, even though it may be a means
of God's grace' (ibid., p. 48).

Finally, we have to consider the End. Just as the Bible
presents creation and the beginning of all things mytho-
logically, so it presents the consummation and the end of
all things in a series of pictures. Nowhere does it give
grounds for a missionary triumphalism such as charac-
terised the nineteenth century. There is nothing to indicate
that everyone will become a Christian; there is no basis for
belief in a conquering Church. Yet the Bible clearly indicates that the victory of Christ will become a recognised
fact and that he whom the world rejects will be vindicated
in this same world and in our history. We find this in the
imagery of the Apocalypse and in the neglected symbolism
of the millennium which Berkhof has boldly expounded
and re-interpreted (op. cit., pp. 153 ff.). Berkhof also grapples
with Paul's curious and puzzling words about the Re-
strainer (2 Thess. 2. 6 f.), concluding that this means the
proclamation of the Gospel (op. cit., p. 130 f.). There is a
restraining hand operative in history which will not permit
ultimate anarchy or a return to primeval chaos. We need
not therefore abandon the too facile optimism of the Victorian Christians for the bleak pessimism of the modern
existentialists and others. We live on the other side of mid-
night. The dawn has come and the light has broken into
the darkness. We have not yet reached that morning without clouds or the city without night, but that is the direction
in which we move, however slowly. It is this movement
which we call the progress of the Gospel. The nature of the
end, like its timing, is beyond our knowing. According to
the New Testament Scriptures—and there is no higher
authority in this sphere—'he is coming with the clouds!
Every eye shall see him, and among them those who
pierced him' (Rev. 1. 7); every knee will bow to him—in
heaven, on earth, and in the depths—and every tongue confess. ' "Jesus Christ is Lord", to the glory of God the Father'
(Phil. 2. 11). 'The kingdom of the world has become the
kingdom of our Lord and of his Christ, and he shall reign

for ever and ever' (Rev. 11. 15 R.S.V.). St. Paul says that at
the end Christ 'delivers up the kingdom to God the Father
after abolishing every kind of domination, authority, and
power . . . and thus God will be all in all' (1 Cor. 15. 24, 28).
We are not entitled to fuller information, but neither need
we live by a faith that believes less. Christianity asserts the
present and ultimate Lordship of Jesus Christ. Our task is
to interpret his Lordship, his mastery, his supremacy, to our
contemporaries in terms of mission and of ministry. We
cannot attempt this unless we accept the stance prescribed
for the total Christian community: that of being *sent to
serve*.

VII. THE UNCHANGING GOSPEL FOR ALL
THE WORLD

IF there are two things above all else which the Christian mission must always be concerned with, those two things are the Gospel and the world. Together they make up a good deal of the theology of mission. They also present the contemporary Church with its greatest and most challenging problems. How are we to interpret and communicate the Gospel? How are we to understand and serve the world?

The Gospel is historic, arising out of certain events, and set out in certain forms of words. While the way we apprehend it and the use we make of it can change, the Gospel itself can no more change than the Norman Conquest or Shakespeare's Hamlet. It is part of the human heritage. But the world in which the Gospel has to be believed and proclaimed is a universe, composed of a variety of peoples and races and cultures and languages and faiths and hopes. And the world is changing all the time, in some places beyond recognition. The whole lecture could be surrendered to exploring this, but as an example I quote one traveller's description of Kuwait, which I can myself fully verify. He calls it 'a concentration of technological achievement—a phenomenal experience of sheer marvel, in the wealth of oil exploitation, the tanker jetties, the massive water distillation, the annual revenues averaging some $3,000 per citizen from one commodity, the pleasant luxury of trees and shrubs along the boulevards costing $250 apiece a year to water, and the generous provision of social and educational welfare in the community, and all within a quarter of a century of a primitive economy unchanging since the days of the Prophet himself' (Kenneth Cragg, *The Privilege of Man*, 5). Our task then is first to examine what is meant by the unchanging Gospel, and then to ask whether and how it can be for a rapidly changing world in its totality. In the

language Paul Tillich loved to use this means the uniqueness and the universality of the Christ Event. And without
anticipating the argument we may notice the hint in this
phrase, combining as it does the One and the All, that only
the unique can make claims to universal attention and relevance.

However much the New Testament writers may differ in
their approach, their comprehension, and their use of
words, they are all agreed on the unique character and the
total significance of the Event they are recording and the
Man they are portraying. In modern biblical scholarship
this is beyond dispute. The classical expression of this
apostolic conviction is found in Paul's letter to the Galatians. After the formal greetings he comes to the point at
once, expressing astonishment that they are turning to 'a
different gospel—not that there is another gospel'. Twice he
anathematises anyone who should preach 'a gospel contrary
to that which you received' (1. 6–9). He insists that the
gospel is 'no human invention'; it came to him through
revelation. On a visit to Jerusalem many years later he laid
this gospel before the men of repute, presumably a caucus
of the apostles; the only distinction recognised was not between Paul's gospel and theirs, the earlier tradition, but between those to whom Paul was sent, the Gentiles, and those
to whom Peter was sent, the Jews. On the celebrated occasion of controversy at Antioch, Paul made an issue out of
the apartheid tendencies of Peter and his colleagues because 'their conduct did not square with the truth of the
Gospel' (2. 14). In other words the Gospel is noted not for its
flexibility in a variety of human situations but for a fixity
which makes it applicable to all situations. Part of the
greatness of St. Paul was first, that he grasped this clearly
and so refused to dilute or adapt or compromise the heart
of the Gospel, and second, that he saw that the essential
Christian experience could result only from the Gospel.
'You stupid Galatians! ... Answer me one question: did
you receive the Spirit by keeping the law or by believing the
gospel message?' (3. 1, 2). This first part of *Galatians* demonstrates how in the apostolic Church the Gospel, long before
there were written gospels, provided a norm, a criterion, a
standard, not only for belief but also for conduct and even

for experience.

We find a similar concern about the nature of the Gospel in 1 Corinthians 5. 1–2. The apostle says he must remind them of the Gospel he had preached to them. He goes on to indicate that they, the Christian community, have a three-fold relation to the Gospel. They received it; they took their stand on it; and it is now bringing them salvation. In other words, there had been a preaching and an acceptance by faith; the Gospel had proved to be the foundation of their new social and personal Christian life; and it continued to link them on to the power of the salvation-experience in every variety of circumstance. But there is a condition attached—'if you hold it fast'.

It is possible—and it would not be surprising—that some of you are beginning to think, either with relief or despair, that I am quoting these passages to support an old-fashioned conservative position. Such a conclusion would be premature. In a remarkable exposition of the phrase 'another gospel' Karl Barth says that this kind of falsification 'does not usually spring from an evangelical radicalism but from a very unevangelical conservatism'. He maintains that the starting-point of all the great heresies, from ancient Gnosticism to modern rationalism, empiricism, existential-ism, is 'the strange illusion that the Gospel is a tolerably well-known magnitude, a sum of dogmas, forms of life, ideals and hopes prescribed in the Bible ... and as such an object which can be surveyed and considered as such, weighed against the demands of the general spiritual or other situation of a given age, translated into the language and concepts and philosophy and practical notions of this age, and both critically and positively interpreted, reduced, explained, deepened, and applied' (*Church Dogmatics*, Vol. 4, Part 3, p. 818 f.). He calls this indolence, for it regards the Gospel as an object readily accessible and therefore not conceivably the Word of the living God. This is the way to a deformation of the Gospel, a secularised Gospel, another Gospel. The Gospel is not merely a word about Jesus Christ but the Word of Jesus Christ, the Yes of God in him, an eternal Subject 'which reveals itself afresh and establishes fresh knowledge in every age'. Barth sees the Gospel as documented in the Bible and confirmed by the Church but not imprisoned in either. The Church cannot master or possess the Gospel; the Gospel must master and possess the Church. Once the Christian community has lost the Gospel it has also lost the content of its task. I have quoted Barth at this point, not as one of his disciples, but to show that faithfulness to the primacy of the Gospel is not necessarily to be equated with theological conservatism. In the world of today the Gospel remains far the most radical force to be reckoned with, the originator of all the revolutions which seek to displace it—and their survivor. It is when the Gospel is debased into a new law that its eternal vitality is sapped and the church which has misused it begins to wither.

What then do we mean by the Gospel? I have come to believe that this is the most crucial theological question of our generation. On the one hand it is not something that can be reduced to a formula or a series of statements; it is not purely historic in the sense that Magna Carta or the Bill of Rights are historic. We have to take Barth's protest seriously because Jesus Christ is not just a figure of history but is risen, alive, active, and sovereign today, as yesterday and tomorrow and for ever. It is this that constitutes the eternal freshness and the continually new surprises of the Gospel as it confronts us differently from our fathers and the Victorians and the Reformers and St. Bernard and St. Jerome and the rest. Church history suggests that no-one is likely to state the Gospel in a form which will be valid and exhaustive for all time, let alone for all societies. This we have to admit; and the weakness of some conservatives, whether catholic or evangelical, is the desire to perpetuate particular phrases or emphases which may no longer speak to men or be gospel for them. This tendency arises from too close an identification of form and content—the old problem. It is here that some of the radical theologians most deserve to be listened to. As Ian Ramsey, Bishop of Durham, pointed out in an article in *The Times* (Aug. 1968), there are 'two features which the new theology has brought back into the forefront of Christian thinking—a sense of mystery and a theological humility'. It is not enough to confine the element of mystery to the sacraments. There is mystery in the Word also. The only alternative to the miraculous in the almost mechanical sense or the memorialist in the purely historic sense is the mysterious in the dynamic sense.

Yet, on the other hand, we cannot evade the fact that apart from certain events in history there would be no Gospel, or at least it would not be known to men. For the Gospel is not just about divine attitudes; it is about divine action. The action took place in world history. It is well authenticated in the documents of the New Testament. There is general agreement about what happened and what it meant, though there is great variety in the manner of presentation by the New Testament writers. This need not imply that no-one is entitled to see meanings in the Christ-event which were not apparent to the New Testament writers, living as they did in an age so different from our own; but it certainly does imply that we are not free to pick and choose, that we cannot treat either the history or the records in a cavalier manner, discarding the inconvenient and the uncomfortable and those elements which offend modern taste or challenge human arrogance. The Gospel is anchored to history and its basic contents cannot be modified if we are still to be left with anything recognised as Gospel. It is here that the conservatives are in a strong position and the radicals are vulnerable. In this connexion the report of the Evangelical Alliance's Commission on Evangelism, *On the Other Side*, deserves study in circles much wider than those that belong to that school of thought. It carefully distinguishes the Gospel from the whole Christian faith; it even distinguishes the irreducible minimum of the Gospel required for saving faith from the full Gospel. But it asserts—rightly in my view—that 'The Gospel is described in the New Testament as the "Gospel of God". It is neither the invention nor the possession of man; it is God's. It is therefore not pride or obstinacy which makes us declare categorically that the essence of the Gospel can neither be reduced nor altered. It is a humble recognition of the fact that the Gospel is God's, and is therefore true for all men and for all time' (p. 68).

Having noticed two different approaches, both with considerable followings today, we have still to answer the question What is the Gospel? I do not propose to engage in exploring the etymology of the word, or to trace its use in the Bible, or to give a summary of the apostolic kerygma. All this may be taken as sufficiently familiar. But current discussion would seem to indicate that the Gospel has to be understood in three categories: in history, in language, in experience—or, if you prefer it, in the existential sphere.

Its historic character we have already noted. Old Testament prophets had looked forward to a new age when messengers would bring good news and human longings would be fulfilled, when a herald would announce 'Here is your God' (Isa. 40. 9 Jerusalem Bible). This new happening occurred with Jesus. He came 'preaching the Gospel of God' (Mk. 1. 14). Here is a fact of history which few would doubt. But those words of Isaiah, 'Here is your God', were taken up by John the Baptist, 'There is the Lamb of God', and by the fourth evangelist in the profoundest theological sense. So the Gospel was not just what Jesus preached; it was also what he embodied. He preached the Kingdom, but he himself was the Kingdom. He announced the good news, but the early Church soon came to see that he was himself the good news. The Gospel he preached came in words and deeds. He had good things to say and good things to do. We need not elaborate on the preaching and teaching or on the mighty works of healing. These were part of his Gospel. But the fulness of the Gospel was only achieved in his death and resurrection in which God was reconciling the world to himself. John Marsh in the fascinating introduction to his Pelican Commentary on St. John draws a distinction between what takes place and what goes on. History as annals describes what took place. But the historian has to make some attempt to say what was going on in what was taking place (p. 18). There is no doubt that Jesus was crucified and that shortly afterwards his disciples believed him to be alive again. Christians, following the apostles, see God's redemptive work going on in man's discreditable part in the passion narrative. With the gift of Pentecost and the availability of the Spirit in the community to interpret the meaning of Jesus Christ, apostolic reflection soon came to focus more and more on the Cross and Resurrection as the centre and pivot of the Gospel. David Jenkins has written: 'Christianity is based on indisputable facts ... I do not say that Christianity is the indisputable interpretation of these facts' (quoted in C. F. D. Moule: *The Phenomenon of the New Testament*, p. 3). Professor Moule admits that what Christians alleged of Jesus is something that cannot be confined within historical terms, and yet, though transcending history 'it is rooted in history and is something to which eye-witness is borne—appeal to eye-witness being an essential part of the early Gospel. Although it cannot be formulated without the use of "trans-historical" terms, yet the historical terms are also essential; and, moreover, the New Testament writers know the difference between the two' (ibid., p. 20). Here, of course, he boldly parts company with the Bultmann school and all who regard the New Testament writers as naïve at this point.

The second category in which the nature of the Gospel has to be discussed is that of language. Words are still indispensable for most forms of communication. The Gospel needs words for its transmission. But words themselves are symbols, and as such vehicles of a greater reality. Jesus used stories to convey the good news. The Gospel itself can be presented as a story and often has been. 'Tell me the old, old story', 'I love to hear the story', 'There's a story to tell to the nations'; these are hymns, perhaps less frequently sung today, that stress this. Paul writing to the Corinthians refers to 'the word of the Cross' and remarks that when he came among them he 'decided to know nothing except Jesus Christ and him crucified'. This must have included the telling of the story and the drawing out of its meaning in certain affirmations such as, 'Christ died for our sins', 'God was in Christ', 'Jesus is Lord', 'The Son of God loved me and gave himself for me'. But the words themselves are not sacrosanct. Their meanings change over the generations. Few people, for example, use the word 'miserable' today in the same sense that it had when the compilers of the Prayer Book used it four hundred years ago. The Gospel has to be translated into other languages and a familiar missionary problem arises when a language contains no suitable word for God. Again, phrases and images which hold deep meaning and elicit real response in one generation or culture are found to be almost useless in another. This was already happening within the New Testament. Expressions such as 'Kingdom of heaven' or 'Son of Man', which could be used among Jews brought up on the Old Testament, had to be discarded by Paul in his Gentile mission because they would have meant nothing. Likewise the Johannine imagery is very different from that of the Synoptists. Nevertheless, although the vehicles or presentation vary, they are controlled by the overwhelming reality of what it is they are presenting. It is this that accounts for the fundamental unity of the New Testament behind the welter of images.

The development of Christian doctrine, and above all the doctrine of the Atonement, demonstrates conclusively the limited duration and value of certain patterns of thought and language. The most recent examination of this problem will be found in F. W. Dillistone's *The Christian Understanding of Atonement.* One of the most famous treatises on the Atonement is Anselm's *Cur Deus Homo?* In the intellectual world of medieval Christendom he must have done more than anyone to interpret the central theme of the Gospel. In the midst of feudal society it was entirely natural to think in terms of honour and satisfaction, debt, and merit. But this set of ideas failed to survive with the passing of feudalism despite Calvin's use of them and their consequent place in reformed theology and even in the Book of Common Prayer. For the most part they certainly will not do today. That is why the supreme task of the theologian and the preacher is to find language which will convey contemporary meaning and not be merely archaeological. Hence all the debate about God-talk and the plea that those who speak in the name of God should use words sensibly and where possible employ models. There is time to give only one example of a constructive approach to this problem and it comes from the book by Georges Velten: *Mission in Industrial France.* Writing about children and youth he observes that they are not noticeably ready to listen to the story of God's concern for mankind or that of Jesus of Nazareth. He then says: 'It is possible for any secular mind, child or adult, to become vitally interested in Jesus, so long as his words and his deeds are reported in secular language and parallels are drawn between his time and ours: between the Samaritans and today's non-churchgoers, between the lepers and maybe today's alcoholics, between the woman of Sychar exhausted by having to walk so far to draw water and present-day families having to share one tap between ten families, because they live on the one landing in the same Paris tenement. Then it becomes apparent to the agnostic child that Jesus is someone who puts human lives straight, giving back to people their human dignity, freeing them from the consequences of their sufferings or their misbehaviour, breaking barriers between social and religious groups. In fact the child can see all this taking place in the club and the centre' (p. 70).

This reference to seeing what is taking place at the club or centre brings us to the third category in which the Gospel has to be considered: experience. In the New Testament the Gospel was not just something that happened in history, or a story that could be put into words; clearly it was a source of power which had never been seen before. We need only quote St. Paul's classic assertion: 'I am not ashamed of the Gospel. It is the saving power of God for everyone who has faith—the Jew first, but the Greek also' (Rom. 1. 16), and Christ crucified he calls 'the power of God and the wisdom of God' (1 Cor. 1. 24). Whether modern Christians still believe that the Gospel has such power, both in a community and in the life of the individual, will decide the future role and impact of the Church on the world far more than all our internal reforms and ecumenical ventures, important as these are. It was almost certainly one aspect of this concern which accounted for the predominant influence at the Uppsala Assembly of the World Council of Churches. We shall return to this shortly; what we are emphasising here is the need for more congregations and communities to demonstrate in their corporate life the power of the Gospel. 'The kingdom of God does not consist in talk but in power,' says Paul (1 Cor. 4. 20). Yet even those with the most sober estimate of the results of the Christian mission in the world must acknowledge that there are enough communities of this kind in almost every country to justify the claim that the Gospel is still the saving power of God.

We have tried to offer some clues towards an answer to the question What is the Gospel? in the three overlapping categories of history, language, and experience. While the Gospel cannot change, man's understanding of it can, and so does the manner of his response. This comes about because of the changing world, and it has two effects. First, we can notice a discarding of what does not essentially belong. Second, there is a new focusing on what may have been neglected. We need not spend time on the first: the work of isolating the kerygma from the total corpus of Christian belief has been done by C. H. Dodd and taken further by Bultmann and others, some would say too far. It also necessitates a clear distinction between the Gospel and civilisation. This had been insufficiently heeded in its proclamation in non-western cultures, and for many in Africa the Gospel is basically associated less with good news of God's love than with the missionaries' apparently harsh insistence on the abandonment of polygamy and in an earlier generation of nakedness. This is as remote from the Gospel as is the length of boys' hair or girls' skirts in the West, and it turns the Gospel into a new law.

But the main challenge of today is whether those who believe the Gospel are prepared to focus it upon the three great issues of our age: war, race, hunger. Here the voice of Uppsala was decisive. No-one who heard him will ever be able to forget the American Negro writer, James Baldwin, saying: 'If you are born under the circumstances in which most black people are born ... the destruction of the Christian Church as it is at present constituted may not only be desirable but may be necessary.' Nor will we forget the brilliant and impassioned speech of Barbara Ward: 'Where, in heaven's name, can we discover any limit to a divine purpose that the wide bounty of the universe has been designed chiefly to benefit 20 per cent of its inhabitants? Where is Christ's word telling us to feed the hungry (provided they are British), to clothe the naked (provided they are German), to shelter the shelterless (provided they are Dutch)?' For their real impact both these speeches should be read in full in *The Ecumenical Review* (Oct. 1968). They are tormenting reminders that this is the world in which the Gospel now has to be preached, and any preaching of the Gospel that ignores its sufferings and injustices has become utterly detached from the Christ who is its central figure. Uppsala was right to expose the Churches to all this.

Unfortunately this led to a somewhat unbalanced statement about the Christian mission. The impression could almost have been gained that the *whole* Gospel is to be found in the parable of the sheep and the goats at the end of Matthew 25 and expressed in the words 'Inasmuch as you did it to one of the least of these my brethren, you did it unto me'. Likewise, a non-ecumenical evangelical—and there are millions of them—might be pardoned for concluding that the Uppsala Assembly thought of mission today chiefly in terms of social and relief work, joining in the protest marches, singing 'We shall overcome', getting involved in a score of activities, but refraining from any direct proclamation, let alone evangelism. Let me say at once that any such conclusions would be unfair, as a careful reading of the report of the Section on Mission will show. Nevertheless there was so strong a swing in this direction that a word of caution and misgiving is justified. Meanwhile, the fact remains, as conservative evangelical groups, especially in North America, never tire of reiterating, that something like two billion people in the world have never yet heard the Christian Gospel. Uppsala in contrast to the Second Vatican Council seemed largely unmoved by this. Delegates, particularly the youth, were rightly moved about the two-thirds of the world that were hungry, and by the fact that this two-thirds roughly coincided with the non-white races which have suffered so much unjust discrimination. Many of them, however, were quite unmoved and undisturbed that for approximately the same two-thirds the Gospel was still unknown. A majority of the section on mission actually defeated at one point a proposal to include a reference to the enormous scale of the unfinished evangelistic task confronting the Churches at a time when population growth is so much greater than the growth of those turning to Christianity. The only mention of this allowed in the final report was qualified in a rather curious and grudging way. 'The Church is rightly concerned for the hundreds of millions who do not know the Gospel of Christ ... But that concern becomes suspect when the Church is preoccupied with its own numerical and institutional strength' (*The Uppsala 68 Report*, p. 32). This, I suggest, is not good enough. The motive for evangelism, except where it is distorted into rank proselytism, is not to add to the

numerical strength of churches—which in any case is not
impressive outside parts of Europe and North America
—but to share with all humanity the Gospel of God made
known in Jesus Christ. It is not just that the Gospel cries
out to be proclaimed as music cries out to be played, but
that the very birthright of every human being entitles him
to know of God's gift beyond words and the possibility of a
new humanity. I am not saying that the giving of the
Gospel is a substitute for the giving of bread. I do say that
the giving of bread, which we must give in dimensions of
economic aid scarcely dreamed of yet, is no substitute for
the giving of the Gospel. The Church has to be concerned
always with both—as Jesus was. Feeding the hungry is a
vital consequence of the Gospel and it is happily shared by
many who do not acknowledge the Gospel. But feeding the
hungry is not identical with the Gospel, for even in our
secularised age man does not live by bread alone. Nor have
all the secularising and desacralising processes, which Harvey Cox and others see occurring in the Bible itself and
reaching their climax in Christ, freed men from fear and
anxiety, whether they be affluent or poor.

The Church then is left with the Gospel. If radical pro-
posals about the distribution of its wealth are ever heeded,
it will be left with little else. That hardly matters. There are
other creeds but there is no other Gospel. It is a quality of
that which is so unique that it holds a universal appeal and
place, unaffected by age or culture. The Taj Mahal, built by
an Indian Muslim to hold the tomb of his wife, is generally
thought to be the most beautiful building in the world, and
people visit it from every corner of the earth. E. M. Forster
wrote in *Howards End*: 'It will be generally admitted that
Beethoven's Fifth Symphony is the most sublime noise that
has ever penetrated into the ear of man. All sorts and conditions are satisfied by it.' So today one can hear it played
by Japanese orchestras. In literature the tragedies of Sopho-
cles and of Shakespeare have no serious rivals, and they are
performed by African university students. The first flight
round the moon and back wins universal praise, and
whether it had been a Russian achievement rather than
American would not have altered this. The unique holds
universal significance and value. These examples refer to

things unique in degree; other things approximate to them. Jesus, however, is unique in kind. What he was, what he said, what he did, what he continues to be, all affirm this. In no other way can we account for the growth of the Church and the spread of the Gospel across every racial and cultural frontier. Professor Moule in an essay entitled *Is Christ Unique?* helpfully invites us to interpret his uniqueness in an inclusive rather than an exclusive sense. He does not hold that Christ is exclusively the truth in such a way that there is truth nowhere else and in no other religion, but that whatever is found true elsewhere is included and transcended in Christ (see *Faith, Fact, and Fantasy*: ed. C. F. D. Moule). This I believe to be a surer way forward than some of the relativist approaches implied in certain types of religious dialogue. We must all learn to live in a world of religious pluralism but this need not mean succumbing to relativism or syncretism, in effect another gospel. In a recorded interview Dr. Visser 't Hooft has said: 'There is in our time, certainly in very large parts of the world and unfortunately in very large parts of the Christian Church, an uncertainty about the right of the Church to bring the Gospel of Christ to people outside its own membership. The modern relativistic mood has affected many Christians ... But to my mind, that more or less relativistic attitude can find no support in the New Testament, which says that the Church has not only the right but the absolute duty to proclaim the Gospel to the end of the earth' (*International Review of Missions*, Oct. 1968, p. 445).

We have looked at some of the factors that challenge the missionary proclamation of the Gospel today: the difficulty of language, its historic character, its replacement by technical aid programmes, its dilution into forms of dialogue based on an uncertainty about the finality of Christ. There are other challenges which I have deliberately left on one side, such as the question raised more specifically by secular Christianity of the Harvey Cox school, the 'God is dead' vogue from the United States, and the demythologised existentialism of Bultmann, because these have been so ably accepted and assessed by the Archbishop of Canterbury in his latest book, *God, Christ, and the World*. With him I believe that 'there is the danger of theology becoming assimilated to the world's wisdom in a false secularity, and there is the danger of theology becoming meaningless through not learning from the world which it sets out to teach. If theology would avoid the dangers of a false secularisation the sure safeguard is to keep at its heart the essential Christian attitudes of creature to Creator, of sinner to Saviour.' Those who adopt this style of living realise readily enough that there is no other name, no other foundation, no other Gospel. A stumbling block it certainly is, as it always has been, and the difficulties of communicating it do not grow less. There is however one great difference today. There was a time when the responsibility for spreading the Gospel rested almost entirely on the Churches of the West. Now it is the shared ecumenical task of the Churches in all six continents. It remains the supreme and ultimate task of the universal Church. The Gospel is still the best that Christians have to offer for the wounds and sorrows of the world. And we have nothing else.

INDEX